Errol,

Best wishes,

Diana

Sept 1/14

SOFT SKILLS
VOLUME 1

A Collection of Strategies, Anecdotes,
Techniques, Observations, Stories, Tactics,
Advice, Experiences, Ideas, and Methods.

Diana Kawarsky

ISBN: 978-1-4834-4942-5 (sc)
ISBN: 978-1-4834-4941-8 (e)

Library of Congress Control Number: 2016905117

Lulu Publishing Services rev. date: 04/05/2016

(In order of appearance, height, weight and shoe size.)

Sheldon — You are my heart.
Jonah — I am very excited to watch you become an incredible man.
Sarah — The world better watch out for you - you're going to be amazing.

CONTENTS

PREFACE

Life can only be understood backwards; but it must be lived forwards.

—*Søren Kierkegaard*

At The Soft Skills Group Inc. there is a real emphasis on how each of our clients can apply learning, make it valuable on-the-job and take it along their way towards further professional development. We developed the HIF Principle to guide us in our approach and ground us in our choices.

The HIF Principle:

> Hindsight
> Insight
> Foresight

These are the three most revealing ways to see into your management choices.

> What choice did you make?
> What choice are you making?
> What choice do you intend to make?

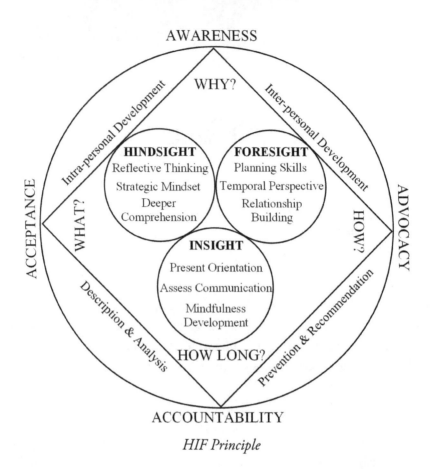

HIF Principle

Hindsight is where we actually have the least influence or control. What ever happened, happened. This is true whether it happened 1 second ago, 10 hours ago, or 100 years ago. Sure, we have our subjective interpretations of past events. But that's not whether or not an event occurred. Then jump ahead to foresight, focusing on the future. How much control do you have over the future? We can generally agree that we all have more control or influence over the future than the past. But does anyone have ultimate power with the ability to predict and even dictate the future? No, instead we have the best-laid plans, don't we? We have vision statements, mission statements, SOPs (Standard Operating Procedures), hopes, strategies, and policies, etc. Even the most intricate and thoughtfully designed plans of foresight get mucked up when we throw those pesky humans into the mix. They can be unpredictable, can't they? But most of us would agree that we have some influence or control over the future, certainly more than the past. We have some abilities and limited capabilities over what is yet to happen. Then there is the insight we can have into the present. And in terms of control or influence that we can yield, well the maximum amount of control is available to us in this very present, right here, right now. Today, I have more opportunity to apply my insight than I did to apply either or both of my hindsight or my foresight. The present, this very moment, right now, today, is how I can best leverage my relationships, my career choices and overall brand on-the-job.

Hindsight is clichéd to be 20/20. I know that that is a comfort to some, but it is not always the case. Hindsight is influenced by the emotional— connections to the event, and how the event has evolved i.e. whether it continues into the present.

Insight has a lot to do with self-awareness and how some of us really do spend a lot of time in our own heads and how others spend a lot of time avoiding whatever it is that is going on in our own heads. This self-awareness is an example of intra-personal knowledge, which is the foundation on which we make our interpersonal behavioural choices in how we communicate with each other.

Foresight is not where many of us feel much comfort because it is unknown despite the best of intentions. It is most often where hope and possibility reside. It is also where many of us can get lost and avoid what is happening right here, right now, today. So there is a balance that each of us has to negotiate between the urgency of the present and the innovation of the future, all couched in the knowledge we have gained, either through qualification or disqualification in the past.

HOW TO READ THIS BOOK

Most people are a wandering generality rather than a meaningful specific.

—*Zig Ziglar*

This book was first conceived in 2014. It was written from January to December of 2015 in Canada, the USA, Scotland, England, France and Spain—not to mention, the plane and train rides in-between. The writing occurred in frantic moments of clarity, fits of inspiration and agonizing struggle with personal expression. What a pleasure it has been.

This is a book written after a lot of thought and much self-scrutiny, so much so that I encourage you to scrutinize its contents with vigour. This book is full of the strategies, techniques, and best practices that make your choices broader, your sphere of influence deeper, and your brand more transparent.

Writing takes ego, and ego is informed by both experience and education. Writing this book is an informed choice to share my experience and education to help you make better choices in the work that you do— perhaps even in the life you live.

Just reading this book is great, but it is not enough. It takes some effort to put these ideas into practice, and then your returns will show themselves in your relationships and career. The returns can be huge. These returns, or dividends if you will, are the secret to your success. It's clear that the path to permanent and positive change is practice. However, practice does not make perfect. Repeat: practice does not make perfect. Practice does make permanent. And permanence means you create habits. These habits or habitual tasks then automatically pay dividends without continuous deliberate effort or extensive application of your will power. The creation of new habits is ritual; that's code for practice. It is also through this practice that your brain's neural chemistry will change, ingraining your chosen action as the preferred way for you to interact with yourself and with others. In other words, habits form because your brain does change in response to frequent practice. Your brain forms connections amongst its billions of neurons; so electrical pulses that travel between these interconnected neurons each deliver messages that inform your every thought and action. So the more you perform or engage in a particular action, means that there are more connections forming between the connected neurons.

The fact remains that each of the ideas that I have included in this book is based on years of what I call "soft skills science" each one lived, talked through, applied on-the-job, workshopped, and refined. Books, which know how to improve your soft skills can be inspirational, but few are full of soft skills science-proven methods, like this one.

Overall book format:

This book is organized into parts. Each part contains a selection of entries that I have chosen from the teaching, speaking and coaching I offer my client groups and individuals. Each of these entries is discrete, but at the same time can conveniently be combined into an iterative reading experience or general learning process. They are darn interesting.

Also, these entries have each been extrapolated from the instructional curriculum I offer and elaborate upon into PowerPoint or Prezi when I speak at conferences. Keeping in mind that I receive performance feedback on my content and delivery each and every day I work, these are tidbits of information that have been thoughtfully scrutinized before I offer them to you, dear reader. It is amazing how generous people are when providing feedback to a Facilitator or Speaker. Thank you to each and every one of my learners and attendees.

My overall intention is that this specific format will provide you with a flowing and satisfying reading experience. You have options. I like options. I hope you do too. You may undertake reading this book as independent entries, whole sections or from cover to cover as a single jaunt. This design is in response to my anecdotal research with the work I have done with my groups. I have asked, for nearly 20 years, by a show of hands how much uninterrupted time individuals have on-the-job to either read or write. It doesn't matter if it is soft copy or hard copy materials, reading on a handheld device, on a desktop monitor, on a piece of paper or on a website. Until approximately five years ago most people would have their hands up (rather proudly actually) indicating that they would have 30-minute uninterrupted time slots or longer to write or read. Since then these 30 minutes have been on a steep and steady decline. This is true regardless of industry, level of authority, years of experience, educational background or work style.

In 2015 when I ask this question the overwhelming majority of individuals tell me that they usually have 5-10-minute instalments of time to actually do their work, think or engage with others before they are pulled hither or dither. And equally anecdotally I would offer to you that none of them seem particularly proud of this fact whatsoever, but that is my conjecture. And while I do believe that anecdotes are not data, at the same time I seem to live a lot of my professional life from one anecdote to another. This book fits into the current 5-10-minute on-the-job landscape we all find ourselves in.

Put a reminder in your calendar:

I'm a huge proponent of using my consciousness for the moment—the immediate moment at hand. I use my Outlook calendar as a means of reminding myself of all sorts of things/tasks/techniques/ideas and best practices. For example, I admit it; my tone can on occasion be less than ideal. I know I have a way of expressing myself that can be assertive, too assertive given the company I may be keeping, or the circumstance I find myself in. I also have a tendency to lean towards the sarcastic when I'm tired or just anxious to be getting on with my day. (Yes, that is a wonky way of admitting I lack patience. Geez, one confession after another. You're not thinking much of me yet, are you?) A private reminder note in my Outlook calendar that urges me to bring my tone to my consciousness, that asks me if I have been patient, or if I have been thoughtful towards others, can change the course of my next meeting or influence how I conduct myself for the remainder of an entire workday.

I recommend you use your calendar and populate it with private reminders that will urge you to move forward, try new techniques, remind you of your best practices, and drive you in your chosen directions. This is a technique that was originally shared with me by one of the very first senior executives that I coached one-on-one, over 20 years ago. I remember him well because he would dedicate a full day at the start of each calendar year to inserting these reminders in hand-written symbols that he drew throughout his hard-copy camel brown leather-bound agenda. It was a gorgeous well-loved Filofax personal organizer. It was a ritual he maintained for decades. And it quickly became one of my own.

I have reminders for many different skills I aim to practice, and I can honestly tell you that once you have this practice as a part of how you organize your time routinely. It is extremely satisfying to have a reminder pop-up that jars your thinking to a better framework, or that corroborates the choices you may be already making in that moment. Choose your repetition rate to suit your investment in the skill.

CAUTION

The biggest fear isn't the fear of failure; it's the fear of failure's consequences.

Herein are techniques that have an impact no matter what level of authority you have on-the-job, no matter what industry you work in, or how much experience you may have. These are the techniques that I offer to my clients in order for the least amount of effort to result in maximized results. Please keep in mind that, while these techniques are valuable to every working professional, how each one is lived can look dramatically different from one person to the next.

This caution is equally important to the techniques themselves. It is the believability factor that is the silent undercurrent to the choices you make to live any or all of these techniques that will set you apart from your peers and improve your overall career branding.

No matter what change you try as a result of reading this book, it will undoubtedly feel awkward or stiff for a while. This is integral to experimenting with and learning new behaviours—you probably know this. Any lifestyle change can predictably feel wooden or uncomfortable at first. Think about starting an exercise routine or incorporating a diet change into your life. New Year's Resolutions are the worst example, but probably the one that resonates with the most people. Newness can be a lot easier to accept as a concept than a practice. So please anticipate mild, extremely mild I hope, discomfort as you try on some of the techniques and ideas in this book. That means you are taking it seriously. Congratulations.

PART 1

PERSONAL MASTERY

CHAPTER 1

COUNTER FACT

Yell "Fire!" not "Help!" if you're in trouble. Most people value property more than others.

—*Maria Lucchetta*

A counter fact is an alternate scenario that your brain creates to help you make sense of or evaluate what has happened. It's a defence mechanism of sorts. We tell ourselves alternate or parallel stories to reconcile our experiences with our expectations. Who wants to be wrong or disappointed anyhow?

You can exercise your power to choose an alternate scenario by consciously selecting a counter fact that makes you feel fortunate rather than helpless. It is hypothetical. After all, the technique here is to develop your consciousness, and then choose what you want to include in your consciousness. You can select your perspective, articulate that perspective to yourself, and then speak of it to others. Ask yourself how you speak of this counter fact to others to solidify or contribute to the refinement of your own thinking.

This is a mental callisthenic of sorts. If calisthenics sounds too vigorous or rigorous or just plain ol' military for you—it could just as successfully be labelled *mental yoga*. Ah, much more Zen, huh? See what I just did? A counter fact need not be grand, complicated or even logical. It can be rather small, specific, and even verging on the nonsensical.

This technique is informed by the psychological idea that one's beliefs can directly affect one's actions.

Beliefs—>Values—>Consciousness—>Actions

Exercise:

Your beliefs are what you use to create your values, your values are what you use to create your consciousness, and your consciousness is what you use to determine your actions.

The best feedback I have had from my clients when it comes to self-awareness exercises is not to start with one's values or beliefs. Instead, pick an action, any action that you have taken on the job. Then think about the story you told yourself about that chosen action—was it fact or counter fact? What would you have done differently with an alternate story or perspective?

Start by making notes to yourself about what you think about when you are engaged in an action or, if you can, about what you think about immediately following. This is about thinking more about your thinking. You'd be surprised to be a fly on the wall at the number of coaching conversations I have had over the years asking clients to share with me their thoughts on their thoughts. It is amazing how few of us actively listen to ourselves and leverage the opportunity to tell ourselves how to think. Try it. This one is almost addictive. Why? Because who is going to think more of your thinking than you are? Think about it.

CHAPTER 2

THE PYGMALION EFFECT

Your success is not a measurement of how many people want to talk to you but of how many listen.

Let's define the Pygmalion effect as the idea that the greater the expectations one places on others, the better they will perform. The effect is named after the Greek myth of Pygmalion, a sculptor who fell in love with a statue he had carved. The expectations we have of our colleagues, our teams, our children, and our partners in life—regardless of whether or not they are voiced—can influence those expectations to become reality.

This is an important idea for decision makers to consider. Asking yourself what you believe of your colleagues, staff, and/or teams can be an important self-check-in, as those beliefs will inform your expectations. Our expectations inform our behavioural choices and the language that we use to communicate with our teams. Do you believe them to be competent? Do you believe them to be motivated? Do you believe them to be of high or low potential? Do you believe them to be sluggish? Ineffective?

If you use language with yourself (intrapersonal) and others (interpersonal) that negatively evaluates and characterizes your colleagues, you are setting your expectations and making them known to others.

Remember, first comes language, and then, behaviors follow.

You were told at some point in time by someone you listened to (for whatever reason—role, power distribution, affection, interdependence, etc.) what it meant to be a good "X." That person's specific language, which oriented your thinking, was a contributing factor to how you subsequently chose to think about your own behaviour and further still influenced your chosen behaviours as either in compliance or alignment with being a good "X" or not. It happens to us all, and it starts when we are young.

In working among these professionals, I ask, "What is the language in your active, on-the-job vocabulary? What are the words, phrases, and sentences that you use to describe and prescribe what a good supervisor, manager, coach, or executive director really is? How do you use this language to identify the behaviors you are looking for?"

Now hold on. Stop here if you're thinking, even for one second, that this is successfully done in an annual performance review, because it is not. This is a daily reality. Language is iterative and cumulative and requires a commitment to create shared meanings and mutual understandings. How many miscommunications and arguments could be avoided if more effort were spent on figuring out what everyone meant behind their words instead of responding to the literal meanings?

Here are the first few verses of the lyrics to a one of my favorite Barenaked Ladies' songs, "What a Good Boy." I often use these words in working with groups of professionals looking to develop their staff and their own leadership.

What A Good Boy

When I was born, they looked at me and said,
what a good boy, what a smart boy, what a strong boy.
And when you were born, they looked at you and said,
what a good girl, what a smart girl, what a pretty girl.

We've got these chains that hang around our necks,
people want to strangle us with them
before we take our first breaths.

Afraid of change, afraid of staying the same,
when temptation calls, we just look away.[1]

Exercise:

Take just a few minutes (no longer, please) and write down, without thinking too much, the words, phrases, and sentences that you would like to overhear spoken about your team as you walk past a group of colleagues in the hall or see written about your team in an email. What language would you like used to accurately describe their work, and vicariously, your work, too?

Once you have the list, you can use this language repeatedly to create shared meaning. When was the last time you spoke or wrote about your team or teams using any of the language that you have in front of you? I run through this exercise in all sorts of workshops on topics like supervisory skills, personal branding, and business storytelling. And without a doubt, this is, my favorite part because when I ask folks, "When was the last time you used any of the language you have on that piece of paper in front of yourselves?" 99 percent of the time, the answer is an embarrassed series of guttural utterances and bashful eye blinking. It's a revelation to a lot of people because they have the language at the ready, but they don't afford the sharing of the language any attention. It goes unspoken unless brought to the fore by an exercise like this one. Using this language requires deliberate efforts of inclusion. Remember, first comes the language, and then the behaviors follow. If you are looking for specific behaviors, be sure to use language that educates your teams and supports their choices. The behaviors will follow.

---

[1] Barenaked Ladies, "What a Good Boy," http://www.azlyrics.com/lyrics/barenakedladies/whatagoodboy.html

THE TETRIS EFFECT

We cannot solve our problems with the same thinking we used when we created them.

—Albert Einstein

The Tetris effect is a great way to understand workflows or diverse perspectives among colleagues on the same scenario. It describes how anyone can get stuck and find him- or herself unable to break a pattern of thinking or behaving.

When your self-talk, mental imagery, and ideas are patterned by a specific activity, that is the Tetris effect in action. It is named after the video game Tetris.

At some point in everyone's career, we work with "that" person. You know the one. The one who predicts doom at each and every team meeting and uses each conversation to corroborate a gloomy prediction of imminent failure. That person who is convinced that no matter what suggestion, innovation, idea, or possibility is at hand, it will fail. This is the Tetris effect in action.

Using the Tetris effect, you can cleanly and swiftly create imagery for people to use. A lot of people will find imagery that someone else has crafted for them useful, as they don't have the breadth to quickly create their own each and every time. Skilled management not only offers team members words but also suggests how they may better think about their contributions to the whole organization. The organic result of providing a familiar image is depersonalization; this is certainly true of any visuals you reference from popular culture. Narratives defined through visual and audio sound bites are sewn into our collective consciousness from popular culture exposure and experience. I would comfortably bet that most people could close their eyes and picture the Tetris game. It is neutral. It is a means of depersonalizing the start of a conversation, which is necessarily personal in its content and intent.

This connects to how many of us hear what it is we want to hear (See Part 2, "Clear Communication").

In a very real way, when I teach business writing techniques, the Tetris Effect is involved. I try to demystify this often-misunderstood technique by breaking it down to its essentials. You know that document (e-mail, report, Web content—it really doesn't matter what kind of document it is) that you have had opened on your desktop all day or the whole weekend or have chipped away at whenever you could, over the last few weeks? That's the document that you've kept in your consciousness to some degree as well, trying to strategize how to write that next line or include a potentially controversial pie chart somewhere. Time elapses, and that document gets stuck. It practically takes on its own persona in your thinking. You've looked at it umpteen times; you've thought about it and maybe even discussed it with your colleagues multiple times, usually to their chagrin, might I add. Guess what? Just as with our own children, we start to see what we want to see over time. We start to suppose that what we mean to write or communicate will come shining through despite the literal words we've written. We're too close to see it objectively. (Everyone's daughter or son is the best, right?) For many of us, the intimacy of writing lends itself to the Tetris effect.

Best Strategy:

Exorcise a dirty, ugly draft of your documents—as complete and as full as you can. Get it out! Get that draft out of your consciousness, out of your head, and out onto a piece of paper, into a Word file, or scribbled on a restaurant napkin. It can become the proverbial monkey on your back unless you let it go. Ever felt haunted by an unwritten email over a weekend, or while trying to watch your young child have fun at their friend's birthday party. Yeah, most of us have.

Change your thinking by changing your perspective on the document. This will happen effortlessly when you re-approach the draft with a fresh set of eyes. As for your children, I can't help there. Mine are perfect, of course.

CHAPTER 4

BUILD MOMENTUM

Your ROA – Return on Attention - outweighs your ROI –
Return on Investment - every time.

The only person I ever condone you trying to fool is you. And this is only because a sucker is indeed born every minute. You can con yourself into doing a task you find despicable, into starting that dreaded filing, returning that email to your office nemesis, starting on that monthly report for your Board that reflects a challenging month for sure. Yes, you can.

But ...

Momentum building is the best way to con yourself into starting, and hopefully continuing, let alone completing a task. This works well with those ugly jobs, organizing one's desk for some, or making that dreaded follow-up call for someone else. Try doing a small, timed portion of the whole task. I recommend no more than 10 minutes. In fact, I find 8 minutes works really well for me. While there are more than a handful of on-the-job tasks I can honestly admit to tolerating, the real dreaded tasks I dread most are in my home life. There's no reason I can offer you as to why, but cleaning a bathroom is a much more tolerable task in an 8-minute chunk than in any other method I have ever tried. By doing even that small of a portion of the whole task, you will feel some progress, dare I say some success even. It is that sense of progress that builds momentum, and will allow you to put together some (limited) enthusiasm. Remember the timing, and move in and out of the task deliberately. It is only 8 minutes, after all. So at the end of the eighth minute get out of there. I mean it. Go! And it feels great on the other side.

So maybe bathroom cleaning is a bit of an extreme example, fine, fine. Think about that report. You know the one, that one you are required to write every three weeks so it can be reviewed by your Director, then given back to you with edits. Then if you're lucky (and the edits are understandable), you return it to that same Director who takes it to his/her monthly update meeting. That report that your Director basically uses as a script because that's how detailed it has become. You know the one? Well, build momentum around your writing. I do this all the time, and perhaps, more importantly, recommend this as a writing technique to many of the writing classes I teach. I have had so many alumni write to me about how writing in bursts is the secret to their newfound writing joy and writing success. It really does take the edge off.

So write that report in a series of timed intervals. Short bursts of writing can create a quick draft and that in turn often makes the whole experience much more satisfying, even if it is the same ol' report but just another month's version. This is true no matter who that Director is, by the way.

Even 8 minutes of simulated commitment can be sufficient for you to put in another 8 minutes, maybe soon thereafter, maybe not.

CHAPTER 5

THE KNOWLEDGE

Know yourself better than a London cabbie knows how to get you to and fro.

Cab drivers in London, England are required to pass a Mensa-worthy qualification test that is affectionately dubbed "The Knowledge."

Unlike many major cities on the planet, London does not follow a grid system. If you've never been there – go.

Toronto, Vancouver, Los Angeles, New York City, Edinburgh, Barcelona, even Milan (sort of) are organized using an overt grid system. London just doesn't and it's amazing, in part, because of it. Winding roads, roundabouts and alleyways abound. Knowing the best route: let alone multiple routes, for each and every passenger from any and to any location in the Greater London Area takes a lot of study and practice. Cabbies are required to know multiple routes, clear alternates, landmarks sights of value and any current events e.g. street festivals or road closures, even construction timetables. And all of this knowledge is required to be at top-of-mind, not maps, and no technology in the cabs. That's right they don't use a GPS even in 2015.

I have introduced The Knowledge to many of my groups since I first learned of it, and most recently upon returning from a European family vacation, making its way into many of my workshops. Literally from Heathrow Airport to our hotel in downtown London, two blocks away from the Thames by the Black Friar's Bridge, we drove past nearly every landmark we were planning on visiting throughout our stay. At the same time, we enjoyed a seriously cantankerous rant on politics and some questionable opinions of visitors from Non-Commonwealth Countries as well as a thorough, and convincing example, of the value of The Knowledge from a native Londoner cabbie. He was more a character from a BBC movie special than a cab driver. Over the years I've worked in New York City many times and while I love Manhattan, I don't relish the cab rides. The cabbies are often hot when it's hot out or cold when it's cold. But more importantly the cabbies just do not know the city. They don't have to, so they don't bother. Many of them are just new to the city and really can't be expected to know it. Not so, never so, in London.

Treat yourself like The Knowledge. Try to learn who you are—look inside yourself to stay current. I hope this small book contributes to your own knowledge.

GET NOTICED:
THE UNSOLICITED REPORT

If you can be that person who helps others make sense of nonsense, your value soars.

Often getting noticed can bring up negative thoughts for some. But it does not need to be so. This is a professional improvement technique to get noticed, shining a spotlight where you want it to be, on your work.

The unsolicited report is a simple and effective way to stand out from the crowd. I have made this suggestion to nearly every group I have worked with over the past 20 years who are focused on learning about writing, and how to get their writing noticed, to bring attention to their skills, recommendations, experience, etc. I advocate that high impact business writing can be ambassadorial of one's skills, experience, accomplishments, and overall promotability. Many folks I work with have been afforded the label of "High Potential." They are affectionately referred to as High Po's.

It was during one of my first weeks working as a Co-ordinator for one of the Provincial Ministries in British Columbia when a Director, rather loudly and sternly to my young new-to-the-workforce ears, asked for an update report on my activities for the month, or basically, since I had come on board. I remember I didn't even know who that Director was until earlier that same day. What a first impression.

So I wrote a report—albeit a flimsy one because, truth be told, I had not done much since taking on the job. I was moderately overwhelmed and (initially) grossly under-skilled. I was inexperienced at being anyone's employee, let alone a government employee. To further complicate this situation, I had used newfangled software; I think it was called something like Outlook to schedule time in my calendar to write that report (and quietly panic). I was as new to Outlook as it was to the work world, certainly to the government ministry of slow-technology adopters. Accidentally (I really could not have done it deliberately if I had tried) I had managed in my quiet panic to set a reminder in my Outlook instructing me to write an update report every month, without an end date. Really no idea how I did that, but I did.

Consequently, being unsure of the technology, I figured that when the reminder appeared the following month that I was indeed expected to write and submit another monthly report to that same Director. Yes, I was *that* under-skilled and *that* green. So, I did what the reminder instructed. I obeyed what Outlook told me and wrote monthly reports, and did so every month for a little over a full year before that Director unexpectedly made an example of me at a weekly team meeting, citing my "unsolicited" monthly reports as an example of my forward-thinking which had distinguished me from my colleagues. I was floored. My colleagues glared at me. My Director gushed. Thanks, Outlook. I was mediocre-skilled at that point, and not nearly as green any longer.

To my surprise, my colleagues' chagrin, and my Director's discretion, I was offered a promotion from Co-ordinator to Manager shortly thereafter. Those colleagues who had been working for the government for much longer than I had were never the same towards me, and rightfully so, as I now had more authority than many of them and some of them were now made my direct reports.

Getting noticed through the unsolicited report has also proven to be effective for more than a few of my clients. I have also heard from more than one writer of the unsolicited report of how valuable a tool it was in scripting a conversation at a board meeting, or in locating appropriate language to deliver reports via PowerPoint to still higher levels of authority in the same organization.

Now, was my rapid career progression in the government exclusively because of those reports? Probably not. I like to think that the work I had completed and documented in those reports were valuable considerations. But those reports definitely set me apart and I got noticed. Consider doing this, if not monthly then perhaps quarterly. Honest.

Being a High Po has its perks.

CHAPTER 7

QUANTIFY

Ask everyone what they think. Become someone who is known to know. Be a thought leader.

Jerry Seinfeld once shared a method he uses that I remember hearing about many years ago, and it stuck with me. I thought it was really insightful into how he manages the sometimes-awkward recognition conversations he has with fans or really with any member of the public. Whether he's walking close to his home in New York City or making his way about anywhere in the world, he is often recognized by passers-by. As his fame increased, he started to practice how to manage these encounters. And he has a method of managing, which I think is a simple one that everyone can use.

His method is to ask at least 1 if not all 3 of the following questions (in no particular order):

1. How much _____?
2. How many _____?
3. How long _____?

So, how much time do you think it will take? How many kids do you have? How long have you been a waitress here?

How long have you enjoyed watching TV? How many times have you seen it? How much do you think that would need?

The secret is to get people quantifying, have them thinking about how much or how many of something; it gets them not thinking about Jerry. And it's the answers to these questions that propel what is sometimes a painfully uncomfortable conversation moving into a more comfortable, de-personalized direction. Quantifying is the key. Although I honestly don't know if Jerry Seinfeld thinks about how people access info in their brains. And for the most part, I don't think much about it either. But I do know that accessing information and organizing it into a quantified amount and then speaking those words, jolts people into a different sort of consciousness. Besides, there really isn't very much to say in response to statements like, "You're Jerry Seinfeld," other than, "Yes, yes I am." Of, course.

I am often in positions where I am in conversations with others before I speak at a conference for example, when it is clear who I am, but the other person is pretty much an unknown. The requirement to chat under the social pressure of possible silence can be pungent. And I use this quantifying method religiously. It works! How long have you worked at this conference centre? How far is your commute? How many people work here doing what you do? How many conferences are held here every year? How many times do you have to ___ each day? How many people are attending today? How many ways can you___? How much time will I need to get back to the airport during Friday afternoon rush hour? Etc.

This is also a remarkably effective technique for that senior level decision-maker in an organization who wants to connect with staff, but keep moving through a departmental visit or while sharing an elevator ride— think choreographed face-time. I have honestly received thank you emails months and years after I shared this method with people about how they use it all of the time with ease.

Anecdotally, I had one of my British clients tell me that he is convinced that the Queen (yes, Her Majesty herself) uses a similar method to keep attendees at functions moving along the receiving line and to control dinner chatter when she has little to no say as to who she sits beside. This makes sense to me.

And wouldn't it be great to out queen the Queen when/if you ever meet her?

Great stuff.

Exercise:

Try it. Asking quantifying questions can get your conversations where you prefer. Act interested by asking not just any question; specifically quantifiable questions will set you apart.

CHAPTER 8

PROTECT AND GUARD YOUR TIME

Better three hours too soon than a minute late.

—William Shakespeare

There are 168 hours per week-every week. And Tuesday is just as long as Saturday. Every Tuesday has 24 hours. Every Saturday does too.

Ingvar Kamprad, IKEA founder, is well known for many reasons, including that he uses his time consciously and with strict economy. He organizes his workday into ten-minute blocks of time to get more done and has a two-minute rule determining his speed and commitment to email responses.

In true IKEA fashion, this is all about the compartmentalization of your workday into small manageable packages. You can then better protect your time from being usurped or from getting away from you unchecked. I guess at some point in time there were questions such as these asked at IKEA: How can we transport this dining room table? What if we take the legs off? What can we do with a compact, flat package instead of a tall and large one? Would this make it more manageable to move? Would a flat package be easier to move? Would it fit into more vehicles? How can this small package make our business better?

As soon as you compartmentalize, even large tasks or projects are made more manageable, definable and traceable. Whether IKEA furniture or your day, when organized into smaller packages it improves your efficiency, then work with one at a time and make the ultimate responsibility yours for your success.

This reminds me of Napoleon Bonaparte's technique of intentionally delaying the opening of his correspondence so that by the time he did, the unimportant issues would have all resolved themselves. He famously would have his mail sitting about in piles. Now keep in mind he lived at a time when sending a letter/message was no easy feat. There were many hands involved in any message getting around, none of it convenient for sure. (But this is the perspective history gives us, isn't it?) Today, following in Napoleon's footsteps, intentionally delaying your response can be an effective way of managing one's email, depending on the relationships with your writers.

This can also be referred to as "limited delay" or "controlled deferral."

Rush unimportant tasks!

Exercise:

Activity Logs

Keep an activity log for several days to track how you spend your time. Note down the change in your activities, e.g. opening mail, making coffee, working, and the time of change for each activity. Note how you feel when performing each activity.

Analyze your Log

You may be surprised to see how much time you spend opening mail, dealing with disruptions, or doing "low-value jobs" in general. Common Sense Skills can be applied to help you use your time in the most effective and productive way possible.

CHAPTER 9

INCITING INCIDENTS & BUSINESS STORYTELLING

The secret of change is to focus all of your energy not on fighting the old, but on building the new.

—Socrates

Inciting is a word from the Latin word *incitare*, which means to put into rapid motion, urge, encourage, and stimulate. An inciting incident catalyses an individual to take action: it often jolts an individual out of everyday routine and into a new pattern of behaviour or thinking. Therefore, it can be the event that can spark a story or a new chapter in one's life. Business stories are not the same as those bedtime stories and fairy tales you may remember from your own childhood, or that you may have recently read to your own child. Business stories differ from regular stories, in that you intentionally craft them and tell them with an objective, goal, or desired result in mind, rather than for entertainment or diversion alone.

How many times have you been captivated by a good story?

Stories are powerful. They can change the way we think, feel, and act. They can form the foundation of an organization's workplace culture; they can turn uncomfortable situations around, capture our imaginations, and inspire us. Stories work differently than hard facts in our thinking; they can illustrate ideas and turn them into fruition through example, and even arouse our principles by engaging our value systems. Stories, specifically your stories, can be very powerful business tools once you learn how to craft them and tell them. It's easy to under-appreciate the influence you have in your relationships because of the stories you have shared and perhaps are known by.

When it comes to business storytelling, I often begin a workshop with two discrete examples of inciting incidents from my life, one personal that I connect to a business lesson, and the other impersonal that I connect to my life. What inciting incidents come to mind in your life? How can you connect them to your business circumstances?

The utility or use-value of thinking about, writing about, and speaking about your own inciting incidents is three-fold:

1. This concept clarifies the meaning from the situation, the wheat from the chaff, for yourself and for your audience.
2. This concept requires an objective narrative-style in order to successfully convey your meaning.
3. This concept liberates you to get ahead of a story, as is often the public relations manoeuvre for public figures to maintain a reputation. It is about building your personal brand.

As a business professional, your inciting incidents can be crafted into your own mantra, effective business stories, motivational examples, and even battle cries to inspire and motivate.

Here's one of my go-to business stories:

Many years ago I learned a lesson that I want to share with you now. It was a lesson in focus. Is your next work conversation about your own feelings or about another person's work? Is it your thoughts/feelings/labels that are of consequence to the work or is it the work? If work does not meet your expectations, is discussing the work's quality (of lack thereof) the point or is the point what you would like to see the work look like from that point onwards? Is it to belittle or build?

I have a remarkably specific relationship with flies, common everyday household flies, much more so than most people and this has been the case now for many years. Those minuscule flies that so many of us swat away have been beacons of personal improvement for me for over half of my life.

It started when I was in my late twenties. I worked for a large, heavy machinery company that brought me on board as a Training Manager. I was young, eager, under sophisticated and impressionable. I was also determined to a good job. I came in early, I stayed late, I volunteered to become involved in additional projects; I was keen, and way, way, way over my head. I spread my efforts so thinly that my actual work was not getting as much of my attention as it needed. My immediate Director had hired me, had otherwise ignored me, and had been too absent in the on-the-job experience to be predictable. She and I had spent very little time together. We had little to no relationship. There was one particular impromptu conversation within the first few weeks of taking the job, with this same Director that I want to tell you about now. She had reviewed one of my recent in-house workshop manuals and she clearly was under-impressed. While she and I were walking down the hallway, she read aloud from one of these manuals of mine and, in a grand voice, announced, "Diana, that is a fly shit point." I was stunned, not insulted, but shocked. I was too green behind the ears for ego to be involved at first—that's how truly under-sophisticated I really was. I genuinely had no idea that she would be so dismissive of my work. I stood there, dumbfounded. And I must have had a revealing expression on my face, because without any prompting from me, she repeated herself, this time a wee bit louder and asked me if I knew what that meant. Did I know what she meant? A "fly shit" point?

With my limited response, she was then both under-impressed and obviously emotionally charged. She was getting angry, really angry, you see I had not reacted as she expected, and I actually had not reacted much at all. Her cheeks were lightly flushed; she spoke quickly and with great emphasis on each and every one of the syllables of each and every one of her words. All the while, as she repeated herself, I stood there in the hallway beside her. This was all beyond my frame of reference. People speak this way to each other at work? I honestly didn't know what she meant, so I said so. This was not the reply she wanted. She went on to explain with the same heightened level of drama in her voice and tone about the minuscule size of the average fly and asked if I could imagine the size of that very minuscule fly's shit. She motioned towards me with finely manicured finger nails a tiny distance between her left thumb and index finger. The penny dropped, along with my jaw. I got it. At least I was a heck of a lot closer than I had been earlier in the conversation.

I got that she did not see value in my work and that her comparison was intentionally trying to trivialize and insult me. I got that she was looking for me to defend myself and to explain myself. I got that the choices I had made in my training manual were clearly not to her liking. I got that we were still in the hallway and that others were beginning to become curious if only because of the volume of her voice. I got that she was agitated and that she was choosing to publicly make her thoughts known, at my expense. I got a lot of things, in a rush of unexpected enlightenment into how under-sophisticated some leaders can be.

In hindsight, her short-temperedness was to my advantage because before I worked up the vocabulary and courage to respond, she loudly and exaggeratedly huffed, shrugged and thumped her way down the remainder of the hall, past many curious colleagues and into her office with a thud crashing behind her as she slammed her door. Whew.

Although she and I never spoke of this exchange, I did make changes to the training manual, and submitted it to her indicating that the revised one would be used from that point forward. Did I think happy thoughts while I did so? No. Did I think about responding to her with equal drama? I did. Did I ever act on those reactionary thoughts - no. There had been more than enough fly shit in the air, in my opinion.

She never acknowledged my revised work. Were they the changes she was looking for? Were they improvements? Were the manuals more effective? I had no idea. Still don't. She never did educate me as to what she was after. And I would have happily accommodated whatever she preferred, I wanted to work there still despite this Director. It was the same moving target it has always been. The exception now was that I had been educated as to how she thought of my work and to some degree of me.

And while I never thought well of her or her communication style again, I have never looked at flies the same. They are tiny, but this story has had a *huge* impact for me.

This is a go-to story that I have offered in many situations with many different groups, for example, it helps me to connect with groups where there may be changes that a team is being asked to roll out - ASAP - that don't necessarily make sense. Or if you are looking for an example of how to make something positive out of what appears initially as negative, this story can quickly get people thinking in the right way.

What is an experience that you have, it can be personal or professional, that you can describe with comfort to others? This same experience has been available to you as a meaning-making opportunity.

Without getting too philosophical, does everything happen for a reason? I really couldn't tell you. But I can tell you that you can surmise a value from any or every experience you have had to create an example of how you have changed, made a choice, risen above the odds, or had life throw lemons at you. Does that mean every story has to include making lemonade from those lemons? No. Inciting incidents are not about rainbows and unicorns, but instead, about *meaning* that you have learned, that you wish to share through telling your story. It is not business story *writing*. It is not business story *thinking*. It is business *storytelling*. You have got to tell the story to have it be meaningful to anyone other than yourself. And in that telling the meaning(s) are often compounded and made more vibrant for the teller.

War stories of an experienced professional are stories, after all, stories that professional has managed to weave into a meaning system of some sort that they can comfortably share. That's it.

When I lead groups for multiple-day workshops, especially three-to-five days in duration, I almost always get feedback from my learners about the stories that I have told as demonstrative of my experience, and how those same stories made the workshop worthwhile. Every story is inspired by an inciting incident that, at the time, may not have been much of an incident at all. It could start out as small as fly shit.

CHAPTER 10

BENIGN NEGLECT

Imbibe the wisdom of others.

This is a skill of some sophistication, and it is only one I recommend when I'm working with senior level decision-makers within organizations who are afforded the liberty of discretion when it comes to their way of personifying their leadership. That's a politically correct way of writing that these individuals must be involved in more of the strategic success of their organization rather than dedicated to the daily tactical responsibilities of profit making. Think: Powerful.

This is a strategic technique that requires one's work to be involved at the macro level as well as contextually parallel to the micro. Big picture responsibilities, which of course, are informed and based on a tactical, small picture base. It requires some level of legitimate authority in order to be career enhancing instead of career limiting. It is neither for the new graduate nor for that staff member who is in a more tactical role.

This concept is more than just leaving well enough alone. This is intentionally and thoughtfully anticipating one's choice of inaction being of greater value than one's action(s). It requires monitoring and planning—strategy really. It is best mastered as a time-bound choice, that is, to figure out approximately how long you will remain uninvolved, and then stick to it unless extreme or unpredictable circumstances arise and all the while you wait and watch.

Benign Neglect is well-intentioned non-interference with an eye to benefit someone or something more than the application of continuous attention might. It is the opposite of Malignant Preoccupation. The classic example of this polar opposite approach is Helicopter Parents/Managers who micro manage and limit the autonomy of others through constant attention.

I have worked with whole Call Centres and in-house with multiple companies in North America with Call Centre professionals; these front-line staff are highly (excessively?) scrutinized. Call Centre environments are exceedingly stressful, and a management approach of Malignant Preoccupation, to my experience, contributes to prohibitive attrition rates. There is an emphasis on the minutiae of task performance and client measurement metrics that could benefit from some distance that comes with Benign Neglect.

Challenge: What processes can you review and wean from your immediate attentions? What tasks can wait? How long can they wait? What do you expect to result from this pause?

If you take a deliberate look at how you spend your time, if you are monitoring and following-up, what would happen if you did so intentionally less frequently? Try this approach. Senior decision-makers often make the clumsy error of not recognizing that benign neglect is a reflection of the skills of one's staff, the fortitude of one's teams, and the strength of the in-place functional workflow processes rather than his or her own short-comings. It is bigger than they are – it is bigger than me – it is bigger than you.

INTEREST PEOPLE BY PAYING ATTENTION TO YOURSELF

Do your intentions vulcanize or galvanize your relationships?

Be mindful, while you communicate, of the overtones as well as the basic content of your message.

Your tone of voice has an important impact on your audience/listeners. While many make the error of relegating tone to a subtlety, it is more suited in the forefront of your communication self-awareness. Your tone can all too easily convey the message that your listeners connect to, hold onto to and choose to identity with rather than your actual chosen words.

How your colleagues know you is influenced by the way you are perceived— this is sometimes called your public image. It is currently trendy in career management circles to write of each of us developing our personal brand. Your tone of voice can tell others how you are feeling, how you may wish they feel, where your attention lies and even whether you are invested in the relationship.

DISTINCTLY, NOT STINKY

First learn then speak the language of success in your immediate environment.

When my son, Jonah, was two years old he attended a daycare centre at the University of Guelph. I was then still somewhat new to motherhood, and very definitely new to balancing work and family. There was one particularly stormy winter day that I won't soon forget when the centre was closing early and all of the parents and kids were fussing trying to get hats and coats, mittens and scarves on the right bodies or in the right bags. It was still tough for me to get myself organized let alone the both of us on some days.

Once Jonah and I had finished dressing and fussing and were ready to brave the elements, we waddled down the hallway towards the exit, Jonah bundled from head to foot in multiple layers, and me carrying multiple bags and backpacks and toys. Neither of us were looking forward to exiting the building very much.

As we approached the exit, we passed a particularly frazzled Mom who was trying to get a left boot onto the right foot of her particularly squirmy two-year-old daughter. This little girl was not having any part of footwear that day, as I had witnessed her removing both her shoes and socks as I had arrived almost thirty minutes prior. And she had not been particularly quiet about her discontent, whatsoever, much as she had many times previously when I was there to pick up Jonah. As we walked by, under the yelps of the squirming two-year-old I overheard that Mom trying to explain in hushed tones, "I said distinctly, honey. Not stinky. You're not stinky." And I laughed out loud. Too loud. I immediately got the dreaded mother-on-mother *malocchio*.

Her words have stayed with me for many years as I have worked them into more than one workshop. She was trying to be as clear as she could with her daughter; she was *distinctly* trying to make a point of clarification. But, her choice of language was totally off the mark. That two-year-old had no idea what her Mom was getting at, and to this little girl's immense credit she tried to interpret to make the most sense of the little sense that had been offered to her in her mother's words. The word 'stinky' makes a lot of sense where you're two. Distinctly is a word that can be confusing for some fifty-year-olds.

Who are you speaking to? Know your audience. It is such a seductive communication error to flex one's vocabulary when what is most appreciated is clarity.

The most brilliant people on the planet are so very often not known as such because they make their knowledge exclusive through their choice of complicated, perhaps even elite language. It is that brilliant person who can distil complexity to a simple and digestible morsel who is better understood and certainly more admired. You can be that person.

LIFE PURPOSE

In school learn how to impress others. In business learn how to express yourself.

"What is your life purpose?" Most people literally have no idea what their purpose is being on this planet. As a result, there can be little direction and diffused enthusiasm in their lives. There seems to me that there is room for improvement here. Think about it.

Here are some examples of Life Purposes, some specific some general:

> To become an outstanding human
> To master my field
> To change the world
> To focus on my personal relationships
> To achieve many small tasks, leading to a larger goal
> To be a great
> To leave a legacy
> To enjoy myself
> "To thine own self be true" as William Shakespeare, wrote.
> "To thine purpose be true" as Diana Kawarsky, wrote.

What is the purpose of your current role at work? This is rarely a replica of your job description. What is your purpose in your family right now? What is the purpose you have for the time you spend with your children, friends or yourself? Think about it. Unfocussed time can easily add up to regrets. Focussed time adds up to our purposes being in our consciousness and much more likely achieved.

Exercises:

Take a few minutes to yourself. This works really well when you are temporarily captive, think flying to your annual conference or that next business trip when you have thirty minutes or so to yourself. I recommend earphones, sunglasses and a hat when traveling.

Think about these questions, write down, or record the immediate responses that come to mind, limit your self-censor. The answers are for your eyes only, so be as brutally honest with yourself as you can bear.

Your *Purpose* Exercise:

Write down the three most important things you do at work.

A clear purpose is an absolute prerequisite for greatness in any aspect of life.

Your *Purposes* Exercise:

This is easily one of my top five favourite exercises to ask a group to experience. I use this two-step exercise in my corporate work to flush out the connectedness or sometimes the disconnectedness of an individual's work to their team, a team to their division, and perhaps, a division to an organization's mission statement or vision statement.

Steps:

> What is the purpose of your job?
> What is your purpose in your job?
> What is the purpose of your team?
> What is the purpose of your direct report(s)?
> What is the purpose of your Director?

These generic questions are just as significant as your specific replies.

Try it. This can also be a great way to have work colleagues improve productivity—respond to the questions individually, and in that case, then come together and compare. There can be some stark differences and overwhelming similarities that rise to the fore.

T SHAPED KNOWLEDGE

You have a thesis. You follow it with an antitheses. If you're
lucky, you reach synthesis. This is knowledge acquisition.

Since the early 2000s, I have heard many people speak of seeking to be more "T" shaped in their knowledge or seeking to recruit more "T" shaped professionals for their teams. I have worked with several Universities in Southern Ontario that have had this letter behind a lot of the discussions determining which professional development topics to include/exclude from their next year calendar offerings. Yes, the letter 'T'.

This is certainly a Google-able topic. Check it out.

Basically, this "T" shape is understood as the vertical stem representing the foundation: an in-depth specialized knowledge in one or two fields. The horizontal crossbar represents the complementary skills of communication, the ability to apply knowledge across disciplines, and a wide-ranging understanding of fields outside your area of expertise. So, you can think of one as depth and the other as breadth.

My work through The Soft Skills Group Inc. is in the breadth crossbar of the "T." Your interest in reading this book is the same.

Although I am reluctant to suggest anyone aspire to be more like any one specific letter of the alphabet, there are 26 choices, after all, the idea of focussing on both one's depth of expertise and breadth of application does resonate with me in my own personal development. I hope it sparks some thoughts for you, too.

CHAPTER 15

MINDFULNESS IS PURPOSEFULNESS

No matter where you go or what you do, you live your entire life within the confines of your head.

—*Terry Josephson*

The act of being present is currently very popular in corporate training circles and management studies.

It is popular because it has wide-reaching applicability to everyone's or anyone's work. And, no, it need not be overwhelming or distracting. Mindfulness is not a make-work project; instead it is a complementary or perhaps a subsidiary range of skills that can keep you engaged - in the moment - this very moment. It is really a way to keep your head in the game, or so the cliché goes. Being engaged, in the moment, aware of one's self, and how one is choosing to interact with the immediate environment, including others, are the primary tenets of mindfulness.

Bringing that awareness of the mind to your consciousness can be done by bringing awareness to how you are intentionally holding your body. What does that mean for you?

A simple and effective technique for increasing your mindfulness is what I call the "Shove Forward & Perk Up."

The Shove Forward & Perk Up Technique:

When seated, and at your next important business meeting, for example, immediately before speaking, gently shove yourself forward on your seat to about the front 1/2 or 1/3. As soon as you do so your back is taller, your shoulders square off, your lung capacity increases, your breathing deepens, you will plant your feet more firmly on the floor and, I'm not sure why, but to top it all off, almost everyone instantaneously smiles widely. I think the smiling has something to do with how using one's body to corroborate one's thoughts is immediately self-satisfying. People then tend to appear quite pleased with themselves. It's attractive. It is a quiet and intense satisfaction that I also think most of us can't even articulate—it's the perk up part of this technique. It's a mood boost without any caffeine.

This 'shoved to the front of your seat' sitting position is mildly (hopefully extremely mildly) uncomfortable for you to do. Plus you are not going to want (perhaps even be physically capable) of maintaining this deliberate posture for extended periods of time. You will experience this new consciousness you've dedicated to how you're holding your body immediately permeate your thoughts. It is the body leading the mind into the moment. A purposefulness in the body is swiftly followed by a purposefulness in the mind - every time.

While in this sitting position you will engage your self-censor; self-edit, cull your thoughts, and become remarkably frugal with your spoken language. In other words, we perk up and are in the moment. It is a calm, private way of having a proverbial bucket of ice water thrown on you. You wake up, even from the dullest of meetings. You recognize your environment: the here and now moment. Once you are done speaking, you can then return to your original, more relaxed position occupying the whole seat. You will feel the relaxation fill your body and your thinking be seasoned with a literal, "ahh … that's more like it" series of thoughts.

This little technique is directive but sincerely non-prescriptive at the same time. It does not dictate what you must or should think about to qualify as mindful. It does not require or recommend a mantra, nor does it require much practice. Instead, this technique is asking you to be in your body, in your immediate environment with thoughtful intention. As a result, your mind de-clutters; focusing you on the present moment of positioning your body, aligning your thoughts, and ultimately in the words you choose to speak.

CHAPTER 16

BECOME A STUDENT OF PSYCHOLOGY

Homogeneous knowledge is secure and can be boringly consistent and unremarkable. Heterogeneous knowledge is volatile and can be surprisingly unpredictable and innovative.

Your business relationships, like any of your relationships, can improve with thoughtfulness and deliberate dedication of your time and energy. Learn by reading books, like this one. Spend some of your time in the business section of your local library or bookstore and grab some new ideas as to how you can influence your relationships based on what others have tried. Just as important can be learning about what choices not to make and how to avoid pitfalls as a result of your new knowledge.

Read.
Listen.
Watch.
Apply.
Repeat.

You're already a student. Reading this book, I hope, is one of many resources you have accessed, read, considered, reviewed, debated, or debunked lately. And continue to do so moving forward. I dare you. I challenge you. I implore you. This is how to ensure your breadth of knowledge continues to evolve and develop over the course of your career.

I am a big fan of interdisciplinary studies and approaches. I thin'
may have influenced me into working in the soft skills area to begi..
so many years ago because they do not conveniently fall into one area.
Soft skills permeate disciplines, cross skill sets; defy cosmetic attributes
like age and gender. And at the same time, soft skills combine all of an
individual's choices into one interdisciplinary, experiential ball of options
and reactions.

Some of the most skilled professionals I have had the pleasure of working
with or knowing are those who are indeed specialists in their fields and
generalists of life. Read outside of your specialty; a lot can be learned from
history by a high-potential Hedge Fund Manager or from studying the
lessons that Modern Art may offer by that new Associate in a Law Firm.

One of my very favourite thinkers on the planet is Alain DeBotton, who
is a crazy good writer, speaker, and also founder of The School of Life. I
have been a fan of his for most of my adult life. I recommend seeking him
out and seeing how his philosophical ideas can be incorporated into your
thinking about the work that you do. I have often read and re-read his
works for new thoughts on my own, including how to approach some of
my workshop topics, and even how to write a few entries in this very book.

This links you back to the idea of T shaped knowledge from earlier in
this section.

RETICULAR ACTIVATING SYSTEM

The RAS is the bridge between your thoughts and how you understand your environment.

The Reticular Activating System (RAS) is part of the brain that decides what is useful and what is not when choosing amongst the billions of pieces of information in the world. It is the way that your brain brings your conscious mind into some sort of order by trying to make sense of all the incoming data to which it is exposed. It is busy categorizing, and maybe even rationalizing all this incoming data by a sort of informational calm of sort. It is part of your brain that literally sifts through the data that is available to you every day, everywhere you look. From that enormity of data, it is the RAS that selects the specific subset of information that pertains to a particular interest that you may have.

It is often best understood as that "magical suddenness" of everything somehow relating to your new interest that you had never before noticed. You and your partner are pregnant, and within a short time of the news, you both notice that there are pregnant women everywhere, there is pregnancy paraphernalia at your finger tips like never before. You are seeing advertising on the best new stroller on the market, tips and techniques on breastfeeding newborns, how to have a "natural" birth, midwifery, food cravings, etc. How did this happen? Did the universe re-orient itself for you? No.

So a person who has just taken up golf or crocheting will find that there are articles in the paper about golf that hadn't ever drawn their attention before. Or crocheting is the activity you notice out of the corner of your eye being done by someone on the bus you ride, then there's a conversation you overhear about the pattern of the crocheted sweater someone is wearing in your office as you pass by an open doorway down the hall from your office. What is going on?

Once you have an understanding of the RAS, I think that it can be equally powerful to try to engage the RAS intentionally. I like the term cognitive bias because it makes sense to me in how I understand the RAS. I hope it does to you too. Try to program yourself to look for how your world is connected to one of your thoughts or values. I don't know if this is a true engagement of my own RAS, but I can tell you that come every April I purposefully start to think about my father, who died when I was six on April 13th. That calendar month is full of father references that I am pretty sure that I seek out and sew into my work and consciousness. He passed almost 40 years ago, and it is still in April, not June when Father's Day falls, that I notice the father/daughter dance in a movie, that I see my own daughter reach for my husband's hand as we all cross the street, or notice older men in the grocery store chatting in hushed Italian voices and I think about how my father could have been one of them.

Does it happen every April, or do I make it happen every April? Not sure. But I can tell you that at this point on my life I almost look forward to it, it makes me feel closer to a man I barely knew. Thanks RAS.

CHAPTER 18

SELF-TALK AFFIRMATIONS

Begin challenging your own assumptions. Your assumptions are your windows on the world. Scrub them off every once in a while, or the light won't come in.

—*Alan Alda*

We each have an internal dialogue, not a monologue. We manage to somehow speak to ourselves - go figure. And it is this internal dialogue where we tell ourselves how to best negotiate our feelings and reconcile them with our immediate environment.

Notice that these are in the present tense.

Most people simply do not take seriously how important it is to think about how one thinks. The quality of your thinking has a huge impact on the quality of your life, and if you choose to, you can strengthen your mental state through positive thinking and developing your self-talk skills.

Your thinking affects the actions you take or do not take. You are what you think about most of the time. Think about that. There have been periods of my adult life when I have had my thinking hijacked by my own under-skill of managing my self-talk. I remember a time when I was living and working in Victoria, BC how I thought of nothing but how I missed my home in Toronto, how I missed a few select people who were back home, and how I wanted to return. I had limited understanding of my inner language. It was a foreign tongue to me most of the time. I had never thought about how I could choose what I was thinking about as a skill. In hindsight, I think I missed a great deal of actually living in Victoria because I was unable to leverage influence on my own thoughts. I was physically in the moment and mentally in the past. This went on for months before I had life shake it out of me by bringing a series of small crises to jerk my thinking into the present.

Self-talk understanding is a technique I offer to many groups I work with under the umbrella of management skills or people-influencing skills. It asks you to imagine what another person's self-talk may be. The challenge with this understanding is then to speak it, albeit tentatively out loud. This means you are putting language to what you are guessing may be the self-talk of your listener, and then speculating out loud as to what you think they are thinking. This is empathetic thinking; it is a stretch for many of us who spend more of our time thinking about what we will say next rather than listening to another person's words let alone, not only listening, but trying to imagine what the thinking that is informing the other person's words may be. Geez. I warned you, it is complicated, but well worth it. It is asking you to equip the other person's point of view, not accept it or deny it. It is asking you to hear and validate the other's perspective, perhaps before they have articulated it very well themselves.

Self-Talk Exercises:

1.   Positive In and Positive Out.

Try to use the same language on the inside as you do on the outside. This is much easier to write about than to do. Positive language frames our thinking and can create the platforms our thoughts use to establish our expectations.

2.   Affirmations and Confirmations.

Positive thinking is not enough. It is the starting point of a re-orientation to the language that you think and ultimately that you choose to use to interact successfully with others. Creating your own tag lines of positive phrases and imagery can be how to take this to the next level. "I am good at …" Make sure you are in the present tense. Be clear and specific and then like the shampoo bottles say, repeat.

3. Thought Pointing.

Ever wonder why we don't spend more time thinking about those things that may interest us like art, love or a special memory or person? This is a technique that allows you to direct your thinking and to luxuriate in a specific idea or image of your choice. No, it's not "a happy place" although it could be. Instead, it is a choice of what you want to think about. You can develop an inventory of thoughts that you point to one spot, thing, or object that you enjoy. These thoughts are a convenient way to re-experience a memory, ignite your creativity about a current situation or challenge, or even to forecast and plan with relish. The pointed thoughts are how to consciously keep your thinking about your thinking at the forefront of your thinking!

4. Increase Your Self-Awareness.

Increase your self-awareness by getting involved in opportunities to know yourself better. What does this mean? It means taking that ½ day course on communication skills that your HR Dept. has arranged for your organization, even though you're busy (who isn't?) and despite you being pretty darn sure your communicate skills are just fine.

5. Who are You Anyhow?

Any opportunities to take self-assessments, or to have feedback provided to you on-the-job are like manna from heaven for your self-talk development. If you are looking for new language to introduce into your self-talk, sometimes the best place to look is outside of yourself. You don't have to re-invent the wheel; you just have to be conscious of wanting a smoother ride.

6. Gratitude.

It is easy to be grateful when there is plenty and not so when there is scarcity. The importance of your self-talk is never higher than when you feel un-ease. It's in those situations like a job interview, or when you see a tractor trailer jackknife on the highway in the lane next to yours, that our deliberate self-talk will allow us to better frame the situation so we can see the opportunity for gratitude. Sometimes, I know it's been this way for me more than once, you have to scrape the very bottom of the gratitude barrel to find it, but there is always some there. You just have to reach with your thoughts to find it.

PREDICT THE FUTURE
BY CREATING IT

Try to catch yourself entertaining problematic perspectives.

I often ask groups to react to this concept, especially when I'm teaching topics like change management, decision-making, or even coaching strategies. The reactions are always furious and diverse. "Create the future?" It creates a buzz amongst senior decision-makers, as they are often hell-bent on predicting and controlling the future as much as feasibly possible. Then there are the middle managers who are often quite jaded in response to this little idea. They often recount tales of having to explain the immediate future to their front line staff while all the while mitigating the long-range interests of their superiors. And then there are the front line staff who are often just as determined to react with utter contempt at the concept. Predict the future? Create the future in order to predict it? What?!?!

Create the future. How is that possible? When one's work is reactive to the whims of management and customers (sometimes those whims are contradictory let alone complementary), it seems impossible.

Can we control the future? No, although, many of us are white-knuckling our hold on the desire to influence the future. We do so on-the-job through vision statements, standard operating procedures (SOPs), mission statements, goals, target outputs, quotas and/or guidelines. Then we make the curious and necessary choice of including humans in these plans and guess what? Things somehow don't always go according to our master plans. Go figure.

Creating the future means act, build today what you want the future to look like. This is how to predict that future. It means take responsibility for how you live your life rather than having it live you.

VALUES AND VALUABLE

Happiness is that state of consciousness which proceeds from the achievement of one's values.

—Ayn Rand

What are your values? Rank them, and then ask if you are living according to those ranked values.

What are the aspects of your life, which you hold dear? How you choose to manifest, support, personify ignore or live your values may change over time. What you hold dear today may not be so tomorrow. I have few pieces of memorabilia of my father; the one that I held dear for many, many years is his record player. It is a beast of a machine, heavy, clunky and probably over 50 years old by now. For most of those years I thought it was the record player that was important. I had thought that it would be one of the few items I would collect if I had to run from my home during a fire. Then, in an innocuous conversation with my husband I realized that the value I had on the record player was of the music that it played, the way the music connected me to my memories. The value shift away from the physical item to the meaning of the music only happened when I asked myself about this value. The fact that the same music can now he downloaded from iTunes and on my phone in my pocket for me to listen to whenever I so desire puts what I value into much more perspective. Although I hope to never be in the situation, I know that the record player wouldn't be worth potentially risking my life. The music would live on without it.

And just to further the personal learning; the epiphany did just occur to me within the last few years that I do have this music in me. It's a part of me – always has been, much more so than the record player could ever be.

Calendar & Cheque Book Challenge– Time and money

I am very fond of the Calendar & Cheque Book Technique because it is a personal and quick tally sheet of how you are spending both your time and money. I wish I could remember who once said to me in a class of mine, "the time you're born with is all the time you get." It was innocuous at the time, and one of those exchanges that has resonated with me ever since.

As the name of this challenge reveals, review and seriously, take a look at how you spend your time. That would be the clock piece. If you are satisfied that the amount of your time doing "x" is accomplishing or contributing to one of your values, great. If not, why not? What can you change? What can you keep the same? What choices with your time are connecting you to your values? What are distracting you from them?

Then the cheque book piece is both to be understood literally and figuratively. Literally, where do you spend your money? What are you contributing your money towards? Causes? Companies? Associations? What are the values behind, informing those dollars?

Money is a sensitive topic for most of us, myself included. I have a real love/hate with the stuff. Nonetheless, this technique is not asking you to (re)evaluate your relationship with money. Instead, it is asking you to deliberately think about and analyze how you choose to spend your money and how much of it you spend. What is it that you are using your money to do or experience? This initial level of analysis can lead to both short term and long term financial commitments that you can believe in and more comfortably define.

NEWNESS

Serendipity is never biased, always neutral, and seldom appreciated.

Try to intentionally create an impression that you are interested in innovation on-the-job by listening to the new ideas others may bring forward. Every new idea, not selected samples.

This can be a clever way for you to be perceived as interested in improvements and that you are forward thinking. This does not necessarily mean that you will implement any new ideas, or that you agree with them (nor for that matter that you actually understand them). The impression of being interested in newness can be enough to keep you in the fold whether or not you pursue a single one of them.

It is very important to spend time generating new ideas - all the time.

Common Error: "We associate more pain to moving forward on a project, and more pleasure to not working on it." These are neural associations that fire off in our brains when we do the same old same old.

"He who has a why to live for can bear almost any how." Nietzsche.

Ask questions—through questions you find the why. The how will surely follow.

Exercise:

1. Create a list of the most significant people, events, choices, technologies and products that influence your own life and the lives of the people whom you care about.
2. Limit your self-censor and get all of the thoughts your have out of your head and onto the paper or screen in front of yourself. Do it quickly. It helps.
3. Sort your items.
4. Surprised by the results?

This is a brief and important exercise because it is strikingly difficult for most people to list the forces that influence and shape their lives. This is how you can spot newness and at the same time develop your social awareness.

CHAPTER 22

ANCHORING

"That's how we have always done it." These are dangerous words. Be warned.

Anchoring is a fantastic term, if only because of the clear imagery it offers: there is a lot of security implied here for business leaders and decision-makers and that can really help some to get focused. This is sometimes clumsily described as a person being "stubborn." And while there may be little between the two terms that is discrete, anchoring allows us to develop an on-the-job vocabulary. And this vocabulary focuses on behaviours. Simple as that.

Anchoring is best understood as having one's thinking connected or, as the anchor image suggests, tied to a specific point or idea. I have often seen it explained and used in medical arenas when a practitioner refuses to abandon an original diagnosis even in the light of new potentially contradictory information on a patient's condition. Ego can be a dramatic obstacle at times to leading well. Simple as that.

Anchoring can be a strong indicator of a leader's clear vision and, for this reason, is the start of almost every successful political campaign. What are the values or party platforms that literally anchor each candidate's choices? Close to home, what are the underpinnings that anchor your recommendations, your ideas for that new parking structure, how to organize the year-end holiday office celebration and so on.

The challenge is to locate the language that anchors you, repeat that language and educate and re-educate others of how your vision is tied to a solid foundation (anchored) over time.

CHAPTER 23

IMPORTANCE OF RITUAL

The more you perform an action, the more it becomes a part of your psyche, and the easier it becomes.

The quality of one's life can be partially understood as determined by the direction of one's thinking. For most people thinking about an outcome is more inspiring than the process, e.g. writing a book. Focusing on a result can feel much more stable in our minds than the unstable means by which we are getting there.

A rote or routine task can be meaningful - if you choose to infuse it with meaning. Think about religious rituals, some of them make daily, mundane tasks rich with meaning, e.g. prayer before or after eating each meal. Many of us eat a few meals every day!

Habits are important. Daily rituals are grounding.

Entrepreneurs are often the most keenly aware of the importance of ritual in their lives while intrapreneurs are more so in relationship on-the-job time specifically.

Entrepreneurs on their own, small business owners, often find that they miss the habits of full-time work, e.g. going to the same coffee shop every morning or chatting with a colleague about nothing before leaving the office every afternoon. While intrapreneurs see how the rituals of being within a large organization can, by circumstance, prescribe routine, e.g.

attending that Health and Safety Committee Meeting every second month with little action resulting - again.

My husband has often commented on how I can get what he calls "stuck." I can listen to a song over and over again within a pretty concentrated period of time with great pleasure. This is a form of torture to him. I learned that I can access more ritualized movement or thinking, and can get into my own Zen-like state, through repeated music. The music I can get stuck on might be a specific song or a specific artist. I will listen to that music over and over again while I write, think, drive or putter around my home. The practice, and yes, I do call this a practice, of intentionally listening to the same music over and over again lets me get into a space that allows me to keep myself on a flow. My music playlist would probably be embarrassing to most of you; however it is this same music that is the secret behind how I can, at times, get so much done.

Often times there are rituals that we engage in so frequently and have done so for so long it can be difficult to think about these activities as rituals. Give this a try. What do you do regularly or have tied to another task in order to get into that state of flow?

PART 2

CLEAR COMMUNICATION

CHAPTER 24

HEARING WHAT WE WANT TO HEAR

We don't see things as they are; we see them as we are.

—*Anaïs Nin*

Funny really how so many of us are convinced that we are original and that our triumphs and challenges are unique. I remember attending an appointment years ago, with our Pediatrician at the time, when my son was under two years old. This doctor was an elderly man who had been in practice longer than I had been alive. I know because of his limited charm and abrupt chair-side manner, in other words he told me so. I remember him examining my son and all the while he was poking him there, looking into this or that orifice or measuring some body part, he spoke into the air (he really didn't engage with me directly at all) about how all of his patients act about the same. Everyone eats dinner within the same 2-3 hour range every day, he said. Every mother worries about their first-born at about the same developmental milestones and brings them in to his office with about the same observations and complaints. Every family has the same challenges within a few years of children starting puberty and of entering adulthood. Everyone does it about the same way and about the same time. Regardless of skin colour, income and/or intelligence.

I remember this appointment mostly because I was taken aback by how he was basically right. And it made immediate sense to me from his perspective that he had concluded on these themes from the probably thousands of children he had treated and families he had worked with over

61

the years. And there I was with my little son at first surprised to be referred to as the same as his other patients and then taking solace that he and I were doing what we were supposed to be doing, as the doctor understood it. There was a new comfort there that I had not experienced before as a young mother. It was lovely and unexpected. It was also short-lived because this same doctor was so curt and really ready for retirement that after his ramblings he quickly dismissed us both and left the examining room, telling me to book a follow-up in 6 months and shut the door with a "humph" like sound. What a guy.

What is this really about? Well, we understand each other by filtering messages through our own experiences and background. We can sometimes be listening more for what conforms to our expectations in our minds rather than what is actually being said in the moment. There can be a lot of security in each of us approximately thinking we know what the other person is going to say as long as it fits into the framework of expectations that our experience has formed for us. This doctor may have wanted his patients to be predictable, as having so many years of practice behind him he was comfortable and competent. And at the same time, I would bet that when a patient did present symptoms outside of his framework, that he was there and ready for the exceptional. If only for the sake of variety.

Try to think about what you would prefer to be hearing, what it is you are hearing and then see how much of a gap remains. This kind of simple communication gap analysis is done all the time in my workshops. But it does not have to be an exercise that remains in a learning environment. I often use this tool when I am attending family functions and trying to "get" what is being said. Try to engage your analysis skills simultaneously while listening to others. Go for it.

CHAPTER 25

INTENTIONS VERSUS PERCEPTIONS

Your words, voice & tone, as well as body language, need to be in alignment to be perceived as you intended.

There can be a divide between the message we intend and the message that is perceived by others. In my industry, a standard and remarkably convenient way of explaining this divide is an explanation of words, voice & tone, and body language.

As you read this section, it is important to keep in mind that this specific ratio of personal communication 7:38:55 (word:tone:body language) is a historical point of reference that was originally offered to analyze and break down communication in a specific context. It has been presented and discussed as pan-applicable with such popularity (some of which as a speaker I have contributed to) that it has moved far from its origins. Does that make it wrong? No, not at all. Instead, I offer these numbers specifically because it is a meaningful platform to start to think about your whole package when you are communicating as well as a launching pad for further discussion on just what the breakdown may be for your specific context(s).

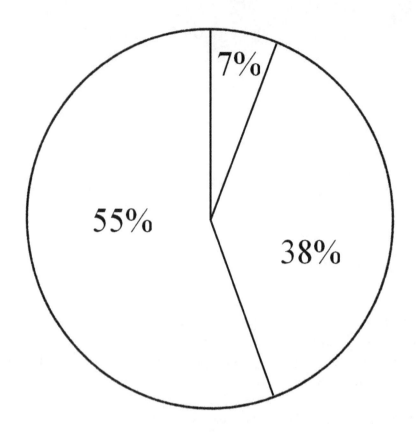

Elements of Personal Communication
(Dr. Albert Mehrabian)
7% spoken words; 38% voice, tone; 55% body language

If only 7% of our meaning is conveyed via our words, why do we obsess over them? Under-skilled speakers/presenters can fixate on their script. Unlike actors, as working professional presenters it's not a commitment to knowing one's lines that will impress an audience. No, not at all. The tonal options and inflections we have with our voices can create the mood, distract your attentions, and strike a much more meaningful chord with any audience. Time and time again, I have lived this and seen this happen. Finally, body language is the final pillar that supports your message.

What does all this have to do with intentions versus perceptions? "Oooohhhh! Oooohhh! Oooohhh!" as Arnold Horshack would say. (I have wanted to include a Welcome Back, Kotter reference somewhere in this book. It took me a while, that's for sure.) The connection is that your words, voice and tone as well as body language in combination form the mental footbridge your listeners (no matter how few or how many) traverse to affirm your intention behind your message and then assign a corresponding perception to it. To have the optimal opportunity, there are no guarantees what humans remember, one must try to strictly align one's words, voice and tone as well as body language with one's intention(s). This focuses your listeners' attentions to the correct perception you're looking for them to have. This doesn't mean to suggest or even slightly infer that your intentions must necessarily be pure of heart, chaste or wholesome, they may very well be malicious and malignant. Keep in mind, the clearer your self-awareness and resultant commitment to your intentions as you communicate, the more seamless the alignment will be amongst your words, voice and tone as well as body language to all support a consistent message; each pillar inline to support the other. And this means a much higher likelihood of yielding your preferred perceptions each and every time. Being understood is about being consistent.

CHAPTER 26

BODY LANGUAGE

We often believe what we see more than what we hear.

Clear communication means listening to the words spoken, the manner in which those words are spoken and watching how those same words are packaged within the speaker's body and their use of immediate space.

Leveraging body language cues is often the reason why that presenter is so compelling, why we believe that politician, and why we may not be convinced that our spouse/partner is being totally honest with us. It packages our words and can be the single most important factor in your overall believability and credibility. Because so many of us carry ourselves to maximize our own physical comfort at all times, we can time and again inadvertently create discomfort for our listeners.

The "how" of how we understand each other is body language. It is the physical packaging of our chosen words and preferred vocabulary. We literally deliver our words in how we complement or detract with our bodies. Impressions come in how we position ourselves onto ourselves alone or in relationship to one another.

Here is what I mean. That woman at the women-only spa. I am fortunate to frequent a few times every year. I am "that" woman. You know who I am. I cocoon myself in towels, an open book in my lap, a pen at my side, maybe even a notepad, a drink on my other side and non-specific-type of general scowl on my face and intentional vacant (uninterested? focused?)

look in my eyes. "Go away," is the clear message, without a word being said. And, without fail, you do. Thank you. Ahhhhh. That's why I go to the spa.

I often ask professionals to see that it is their body language that can be used to leverage one's overall credibility in a first impression, but, more importantly, it is in those habitual impressions that we make with our long-term relationships. There is plenty written about the importance of first impressions – some mediocre and some insightful for sure. I ask what I have been told is a compelling question in this area: How are you maintaining a positive impression over time?" That's what I call your habitual impression. And it is clearly two separate skill sets to make a positive first impression (think: job interview and handshakes and posture kind of stuff) and then to be on-board for weeks or months and to be intentionally perpetuating your impression (think: brand awareness and connecting with other kinds of stuff).

CHAPTER 27

PRINCIPLES OF LISTENING WELL

Get into your head to get into the game.

Listening is one of the most underrated, least practiced, and appreciated skills anyone can possess. Listening requires an investment of the self that recognizes that others are valuable and deserving of our attention. It is also a self-serving process in that successful listening will often result in you having a clearer understanding of your own thoughts and interpretations. Plus it serves to noticeably build your immediate relationship through the display of your effortful, deliberate investment.

Listening requires you to be in the present: in this very moment. It is a skill of concentration in a time when we all intentionally and unintentionally live distracted lives. When was the last time you did one thing? Only one thing? This kind of mindfulness is really tough to exercise in a world that asks for and often celebrates multitasking. The science again and again suggests to me that we just do not do our best when we scatter our efforts. Practicing listening well can mean listening to your own thoughts and reducing the inner noise of your own thoughts as well as trying to selectively weed out distractions in your social environment. There's actually a lot going on. Try this out: I encourage you to try to listen to one particular instrument when listening to music, or one conversation next time you're on public transit.

In yoga, there is a great deal of teaching around listening well/mindfulness/thoughts as a continuum. If you listen you become mindful, if you are mindful you become aware of your thoughts, if you are aware of your own thoughts you have much more of an opportunity to choose them, refine them and replace them. This entire continuum requires you to listen to both self and other.

A wise owl I worked with when I was fresh out of my undergraduate studies and new to the full-time workforce taught me about listening well. Her advice has stayed with me for decades because of how essential and clever it was and still is. A bit of an axiom for me throughout my career, perhaps it can be for you too. She told me:

1. Give a hoot.
2. Remind yourself of exactly what that hoot is - often.
3. Tell others why you give a hoot.
4. Capture words/phrases/sentences/body language/voice cues/tone inflections etc. that make sense in your conversations. (aka "common sense").
5. Focus on how these captured common sense morsels create shared meaning(s) in your conversations.
6. Want to both learn *and* teach.

Listening is often code for patience. They do go hand-in-hand after all. I am the first to admit to struggling here because I do struggle to be patient. I really do. I am so intentionally listening (being patient really) and giving a hoot while leading groups each and every working day that I can tune out sometimes in my personal relationships. It is true. Go and ask my husband, no, better not. Thanks.

It is neither easy nor my first instinct to continue listening after a day of public speaking, or teaching a group. And, I know all too well that the personal cost of doing so can be great. If I don't pull myself together to listen to those I care about and share my time with outside of my professional persona, I tarnish those relationships. No excuses - but an ongoing challenge. I do indeed give a hoot; I'm also tired and perhaps drained after work also. Listening with this hoot-approach helps me to literally jolt myself into that current conversation and not wallow in my own thoughts - to better get myself into the immediate moment. I listen at work because I want the group to succeed. I listen to my family because I hold them as precious.

Hoot. Hoot. Try it out for yourself.

CHAPTER 28

SAME GOES FOR THE PHONE

Your voice and tone always convey more meaning than you think.

From the toolkit of best practices for customer service-oriented jobs, it is very usual to hear that a smile can he heard over the phone. I like the toolkit image as it helps to conceptualize that customer service is reactive and that a different tool may be needed than you had originally seen fit, just as a tradesperson will need to know how to improvise with his/her toolkit. Does this mean we can hear your face cracking as you bring the corners of your mouth northward? No, it means that when we hold our bodies differently; our tone is influenced. When we deliberately choose to position ourselves with purpose, our voices and overall tone are both influenced, perhaps even informed. So, sit up. Your mother was right (at least once).

More than one call centre where I have worked has benefitted from a trip to the local dollar store and purchasing small magnetic mirrors. Staff place them within their own eye-line as they work on the phone, in order to catch themselves when they are not smiling and to see how their bodies evolve over the course of a call from tall and engaged in appearance to slumped over and almost collapsing upon one's self.

When I am conducting coaching sessions over the phone or on any business call of over thirty minutes, I bring out my own little mirror that I position beside my notepad or keyboard so that I can continue taking my longhand or typed notes during the call and also see myself and how I am holding my body. This allows me to stay relaxed and simultaneously raise my consciousness of my actions. It is simple and really works. My tone improves every time. Yours will too.

CHAPTER 29

LOOK INTERESTED

Open your heart to others by occupying your full airspace.

When speaking, be sure to face your audience/listeners, full on, shoulders squared as often as possible or as the physical arrangement allows. This is particularly true if there is a size differential that can be distracting. Face the group, offer consistent eye contact and establish an open posture. If you're of a shorter stature, it is equally important as someone who is taller than the majority of the herd. Everyone looks more interested when they are fully available physically; occupying the maximum amount of airspace you comfortably can challenge your body to fill.

What is an open posture? It means offering the biggest physical version of yourself: shoulders back, back erect, open-eyed, and even perhaps a slight forward lean throughout to indicate your interest in the conversation. Often you will hear professional speakers at conferences deliver their spiel on opening your heart to your audience as well as your mind. This goes back to your body language choices—hold yourself with purpose. What is your purpose? At least some of the time I hope it is to achieve clear communication. And being open with both your language and your body will influence just how clearly your message is understood.

PART 3

WORK RELATIONSHIPS

CHAPTER 30

ON AND OFF

I make my relationships at work.

—*Carol Kane*

It is a best practice to be in "work mode" as soon as you hit the work real estate—virtually or in-person. What does that mean? It means if you work in a building in downtown Toronto connected to the underground Path system, as soon as you step foot onto the Path, no matter what time of day, no matter how near or far from your building or your organization, you are to be intentionally, deliberately in work mode immediately, and until you leave the real estate.

If you work in Boston and take the "T" to work every day, you might consider that bus ride as where your work mode begins. Mobile real estate? If it's your daily commute, chances are it is also for some, if not most of the others on the same route. And the likelihood of one of those commuters being a customer or a contact one day are relatively good. I remind my clients that those chances are not absolute, but at the same time, good enough to validate your professional mode to be switched on, just in case.

There are eyes and ears that can create an impression of you as you inadvertently are making your way along. This is equally important in smaller communities. When I lived in Victoria, BC I remember being approached by a woman on the street with a warm grin and a deliberate greeting. I had no idea who she was. And I was there in my weekend wear, not in any way thinking about my work self.

It turned out she had been my waitress during a business lunch I had had the previous week and happened to live near me and know my lunch companion as well. That companion turned out to be a key contact for me as I soon thereafter networked my way to my next position.

Work mode is an invisible hat I put on when I'm working, including commuting time. Really, this means whenever I may be on display, whenever others may judge my professional conduct, I try to put that hat on. It also makes taking the darn thing off at the end of the day quite satisfying. Even in your torn jeans and mismatched running gear, work mode is how you choose to conduct yourself despite the obvious wardrobe and environment changes. How you choose to interact professionally, despite wearing a T-shirt that says, "Kiss the Cook." It is about your choice in representing yourself well at all times.

When you were a kid did you ever see one of your teachers in a grocery store on the weekend with their own kids, perhaps looking a little haggard, trying desperately to parent? This sighting stuns most kids. A teacher out of their "natural" classroom environment, out in the wilds of the community at-large: buying groceries no less. "I never thought Mrs. Walker would shop for groceries or eat food?!" There is no return to the original unsullied relationship that kid once had with Mrs. Walker. It has changed forever.

On and Off. That kid eventually grows up and now may even be reading this little book.

When I have run into attendees of one of my conference talks or from a company where I may have lead in-house training, it can be remarkably uncomfortable. I am a fervent practitioner of on and off; so I tend to be the one who shines a spotlight on that other person's off with my on. Once in a playground with my then 3-year-old son, I had a man approach me and ask me if my name was Diana. "Are you the Diana that spoke at the blah blah blah conference last year? I sat in the back of the room. You were great. Why are you here?" I smiled and pointed to my son on the slide. "Oh, you're here with your son. You have a son? You didn't mention that at the conference. Well, … … umm (looking around for his own offspring) I'm here too because I have a daughter. She's over there. Well, we have to go … … Bye." And off he goes. I have had this same monologue-style collision conversation many times over the years with folks who are looking at me like Mrs. Walker must have been looked at every time she bumped into one of her students at the grocery store.

On and Off.

CHAPTER 31

BE SURE YOUR ACTIONS SUPPORT YOUR COMMUNICATIONS

Deeds Speak.

—Vaughan Regional Police

In the final analysis, the most persuasive kind of communication is not what you say, but what you do. We are remembered for our actions, not for our inactions. If legacy does not interest you, then think impact.

And legacy can often be the inspiration for action. Although I hardly ever think about the legacy I am leaving, perhaps this is me mentally white-knuckling my hold on my own youth. Not sure. Nonetheless, being remembered at all is a sort of laundry list of actions that one took that are recognized and recorded. You hardly, if ever hear someone refer to another who has passed as, "She really knew how to play it safe, limit her experiences, do very little of meaning and seldom act with any respect to improving herself or contributing to others, let alone the world," now do you? Think about how people refer to people once they have left your organization? How do you want to be remembered when/if you leave? "That Sally sure managed to do very little for a really long time while she was here, didn't she?" Maybe not.

Once again, your words, voice & tone, as well as your body language, need to be in alignment in order for your intended message to be the message that is perceived. Body language is the majority of your message - communicate with it wisely.

Remember the saying "Actions speak louder than words".

When I work with executives and I hear about how they want to do something and they don't do it, I always ask, "why?" And most of the time I am told that the action under consideration would be a risk. I think that risks are relative, and that one has to consider defining and refining what the risks are before choosing. There is no risk of being a divorcee, no matter how you might try, if you don't ever marry.

There are so many nuances to the social risks we enter into every day on-the-job. Younger women often ask me how can I have the courage to speak in front of groups? I always reply that asking me that question is equally if not more courageous. It is when we act on our interest that our true colours shine through. I find the courage mostly because I have redefined the social risk. What's the worst that could happen? That I don't do well? Then I can do better the next time I am before a group. The choice to act will be the opportunity; it is intrinsic to acting.

THE BLACK SWAN EFFECT

Do not suppose; propose.

—Sheldon Kawarsky

The definition of the Black Swan Effect that I will offer to you is this - it is a major event that surprisingly occurs and would have been extremely difficult to predict. It does not necessarily need to result in something negative and, in fact, many Black Swan events have made a positive impact. Nassim Nicholas Taleb, a finance professor and former Wall Street trader, popularized this term.

This effect is often contrary to even the best-sorted standard operating procedures (SOPs) all of which can be found guilty of attempting to predict and, with some hilarity, control the future. The future unfolds as it does, despite SOPs and those pesky, unpredictable humans who may choose to behave in contrary ways. The Black Swan Effect does not predict the future, it does not offer solutions to the future, and it does not condemn the unexpected. Instead, this effect offers a few clear words to use to label and perhaps de-personalize that things may have unfolded very differently than you, everyone or potentially anyone, would have predicted or preferred. This can be beneficial to how the unexpected is defined, responded to, managed and potentially, overcome.

I have introduced this concept into more than one meeting where the experience of the usually well-intentioned meeting attendees of *not* following their own agenda is how to bring this concept into play. That un-followed agenda is *the* Black Swan Effect. It is a micro-application of the effect, but that can be more than sufficient to get people's minds oriented to what is actually happening. And that meeting is not what was the plan AKA the agenda. It does not point fingers or lay blame on any one person or force. It is inclusive and at the same time soothing to what can be unexpected emotions, which can accompany those unexpected situations.

Consider referring to this effect when you're next in a conversation, meeting or situation on-the-job that has not panned out as planned. It can pre-empt finger pointing, blame games and a great deal of social discomfort. They are just three little words, but they pack a lot of punch. Although thought to be archetypically graceful and beautiful swans have an angry temperament and are known to attack humans – whether black, white or Technicolor. So calling out this effect *curtails* its effect much in the same way as knowing a beautiful swan may attack you at any given moment.

CHAPTER 33

TOUCH PEOPLE ONCE IN A WHILE - OCCASIONALLY, BRIEFLY, & SINCERELY

There are four powers: memory and intellect, desire and covetousness. The first two are mental and the others sensual. The three senses: sight, hearing and smell cannot be prevented; touch and taste not at all.

—Leonardo da Vinci

A light touch on the forearm or a pat on the shoulder offered towards a colleague with whom you have a rapport and a usual level of predictable interaction, can be an effective way of positively affecting the relationship. Don't try this with someone you've just met, or with someone you are in conflict with. Please stay in 100% compliance with the appropriate governing guidelines of your workplace safety. No one is to be made uncomfortable, in any way. And, of course, some people simply do not like to be touched.

Nonetheless, when used infrequently and purposefully in a functional working relationship, a touch can make a big difference. I am one of a privileged few professionals, in one of a handful of industries who enjoy a transient exemption to this social convention. Here's what I mean:

Whenever I am speaking in front of a group of about 30 people or more, I make it a point of making my way into the audience and mingle while speaking. This is not an original speaking technique - in fact; it is a well-honed practice by many before me. While I'm amongst the group, I will always create an opportunity to touch someone usually on the arm or on the shoulder. I even have one very popular exercise I do where I ask for a hand (I usually ask for a man's hand, it generates more laughs, I have no idea why, but it *always* does) and then I guide this man behind me and walk swiftly along a meandering path amongst the group as I continue speaking to make a point. All the while this poor fellow is my captive, hand-in-hand we walk through the others attending, the laughs getting louder and louder as we pass folks maybe two or three times before I (finally!) relinquish my grip whereby this man immediately triggers a remarkably fast retreat to his original seat. I enjoy the laughs as I make my way back to the front of the group, perhaps even stopping for a few more light, appropriate touches along the way as we all chuckle and return to quiet. It is the honesty and humanity that a touch offers that supports work relationships, or, in my case gets the guffaw. It is real, sometimes the only thing that can be seen and understood as real in our work lives, as long as it is brief and sincere.

Respectfulness is relative, and touch must be mindful of respecting personal space. Remember relativity as you proceed, as what you would prefer may *not* be what others seek. That whole idea of, "do unto others as they would have done unto you" assumes that you and that specific other share a very complicated and discrete set of values. The world is too diverse to make such an assumption and have it work out. So, do unto others as you do.

TESTING FOR UNDERSTANDING AKA FOLLOW-UP YOUR COMMUNICATION

When you are focused on understanding it is much tougher to be apathetic.

In your next on-the-job conversation, try to make an intentional effort to really understand what the speaker is saying. Testing for understanding is the most convenient mechanism you have to gaining mutual rapport. And, yes, it is as simple as saying, *"So what you're saying is …"* I recommend emphasizing your effort to understand others as a part of the way you are engaging.

This relates to mirroring the behaviours of those you are engaged with in conversation. Reiterating is really mirroring the verbal. Think about it.

There is a lot of relationship credibility in asking questions, displaying an interest in gaining knowledge and validating another person's perspective. By testing for understanding you are doing the communication equivalent of mathematics' reliability and validity testing models. No, it does not indicate a glut of knowledge on your part. It is *not* a display of your possible shortcomings. And, yes, it does instead create deeper shared meaning amongst colleagues and even serve to solidify your role in your next big meeting. You will be seen as progress-oriented, forward thinking and keen. Not bad, huh? Asking questions means that you are open to whatever the answers may be. The undercurrent assumption here is that you do not enter into this with preconceived answers or an agenda to back-fill. If so, you will fail. In the end, testing for understanding is a display of your sincere interest and maybe even your commitment to mutual understanding, which is without debate accepted as a best practice of teamwork in any organization.

Here are some easy and effective follow-up questions:

    i.   Did that make sense to you?
    ii.   Can I explain that better?
    iii. Would it help if I explained more?
    iv. Am I inline with what you expected me to say?
    v.   Is this new to you? Am I confusing?
    vi. Did I lose you while I was speaking?
    vii. Can I say that again to clarify?
    viii.Am I on track?

After thoughtful and careful preparation, have you ever attended that very important meeting, spoke to your agenda item with your preparation supporting your progress every step of the way, felt really solid in your performance and then look around the table and think something like, "Am I the only one here who speaks English?" It's that type of extreme example of communication disconnect that is most frequently the go-to example for many communication courses. And, yes, it does happen. And, no you're wrong, they do speak English. Yes again, to you choosing to pause and listen to that inner voice and immediately checking in with your listeners. I discourage asking for language comprehension. And I encourage you to ask sincerely whether or not there are any questions or if you may clarify or elaborate on what you have said. It's not just in meetings or during presentations where testing for understanding is valuable. It's in those mundane, usual and much more frequent conversations where most of us miss the mark and continue to blather on for (a great deal sometimes) our own edification.

Make certain that every important communication has some follow-up built into the overall design. For example, a simple and effective presentation technique to build into your toolkit is to insert questions along the way, in and amongst your slide deck to check for understanding. This is far superior to the often bone-dry "any questions" that is (in)sincerely and obligatorily blurted out at the finale of most presentations. Too little checking for understanding to influence your group's levels of general attention and comprehension and too late for any opportunity for you as the presenter to offer additional or even corrective words/action.

Ask if you make sense. Correct it if you don't. Celebrate it when you do.

CHAPTER 35

OFFER FEEDBACK NOT LABELS

Perception can define intention.

Please, please please keep in mind that we are focused on your work relationships in this book. Your on-the-job relationships may offer you similar opportunities as your personal ones to practice and apply a lot of the ideas here, but that is not by design the intention of this writing.

Do share your opinions, and at the same time temper your language with a strict adherence not to label or characterize others. Here are five examples of sound bytes of a conversation I have had many times:

> You: You look tired.
> Me: Yes, I am. Thank you.
>
> You: You look tired.
> Me: No, I'm not tired
>
> You: You look tired.
> Me: I do? Thanks for telling me.
>
> You: You look tired.
> Me: I do? No. I don't think so
>
> You: You look tired.
> Me: So do you.

What is this? What is going on here? Really, what is going on in this conversation? Is this a conversation? It is a characterization via a flimsy observation. It's a label. Is this feedback? Is this in *any* way constructive to the receiver of the message? To the sender? Does it influence the relationship in *any* measurable way at all? It is general, vague and keeps the conversation at a macro level where nothing of value can be learned, shared or for that matter responded to whatsoever. It is unanswerable dribble, potentially contentious and accidentally useless. Upon seeing that one specific colleague, you might very well be thinking thoughts along the lines of, "Wow, he/she really looks tired or angry or old or constipated or happy or unattractive or distracted or disinterested or excited or sad or frustrated." And what of it? Keep such characterizing thoughts to yourself within your work relationships. This is not feedback, but unsolicited commentary. No thank you. Remember the value of asking questions? Think about that here. Asking a simple open-ended question like, "How are you?" is bound to yield information that you may then build upon to either corroborate or refute your initial thoughts.

Feedback is soliciting interaction and responding to that interaction. It is about behaviours not a person's physicality or character. Labels shut down communication and can lead to strained relationships. Who wants to be told that they look tired? Ever? Let alone, again?

CHAPTER 36

HAVE A LAUGH

Be who you are, and say what you feel, because those who mind don't matter, and those who matter don't mind.

—*Dr. Seuss*

It's good for you.

There is plenty of non-controversial science that clearly indicates that laughter is good for you. It is good for all of us, physically, emotionally, physiologically, and spiritually. Laughter can combat disease and improve your general health. It is tax-free, readily available and both gluten-free and carb-free. (See, there was a little giggle there that you didn't see coming, now did you?) Laughter lowers your blood pressure and increases your blood flow and oxygenation levels. All good really, I've yet to hear a downside to laughter. Even laugh lines have become a source of great pride for me as I age. Each one a triumph to a good time I have shared (usually with my husband who can be one damn funny guy at times. Thanks, Honey.)

Laughter is known to decrease both stress and tension while also being a significant player in creating a pleasant, general atmosphere or even rapport on-the-job. We become more open to positive interpretation of each other's choices and generally more actively engaged in how we are interacting with others. Lots of good stuff here, really.

If you must go so far as to commit specific time in your calendar to laughing, then do it. This is no laughing matter. So go ahead and put that reminder in your Outlook calendar. Have you laughed today?

I have coached more than one executive who has a weekly (or dare I reveal a daily) reminder set in their Outlook schedules to find a reason to laugh. Real or fictional sources of laughter are all on the table. Whatever gives you a quick giggle.

Go for it.

CHAPTER 37

HUMOUR & SOCIAL RISK

He who laughs most, learns best.

—*John Cleese*

For all of its benefits, there are some hindrances to either introducing or participating in humour in your workplace. There can be a tangible risk of offending others when the humour comments on culture, gender, religion, or politics. There can be a lot of unknown sensitivities that are brought to the surface through humour, and so it is a general best practice to use humour carefully.

Humour is not laughter. In the "Have a Laugh" Section I promoted finding sources of humour and celebrating the effects on us as multidimensional beings on the job. We are not robot workers (yet?). Humour is the source of one's laughter. As we reach outwards or look at our surroundings, we may find humour. We are rather clever when given a chance. Trying to be funny is not necessarily funny and it is not necessarily when you or others will be inspired to laugh. That's the risk, right there. Tread softly.

Humour is the biggest risk.

Social risk - I've learned that of all of the layers of challenge to leading and/or influencing humans none can be more frightening to people than choosing to engage in public speaking. Remember that famous, now perhaps correctly labeled infamous Jerry Seinfeld observation, "most people would rather be in the casket at a funeral than delivering the eulogy." For some, a lot of us actually, trying to be funny is like being in the casket, for most of us it's much more like delivering the eulogy. Either way we all respond to that person who can bring levity to the job in a positive way.

CHAPTER 38

SARCASM

You had to learn at a certain age what sarcasm is, you know?

—Penny Marshall

I am especially interested in cautioning my clients about the use of sarcasm when they come to me with observations such as, "I just don't think our customers are being heard." Or, " I know my team is competent, but it's *how* they communicate that I think really needs to be improved."

Sarcasm can be as natural to spoken language as the words we use. It's a tone choice that depends on one's true meaning being understood via the tone inflection despite the literal meaning of the words chosen. In other words, it is in *how* I say it not *what* I say that requires my listener to perceive my sarcasm as I had originally intended. Sarcasm is a tone choice that for many is unconscious and woven into how one speaks. For others, sarcasm is a complicated and ambiguous language delivery mechanism that confuses and blurs the message.

Beware of your tone.

Now sarcasm is only one example of a tone other than sincerity. Keep in mind that all tones other than sincerity are spoken somewhat slower than sincerity. Sarcasm requires a much slower, and obviously exaggerated manner of speaking because the words themselves are not where the speaker's true meaning lies. Ever listen to the average teenager say something like, "Yeeeeeeees, Mommmmmm." Sarcasm at its finest.

CHAPTER 39

USE A POSITIVE, TACTFUL TONE

We often refuse to accept an idea merely because the tone of voice in which it has been expressed is unsympathetic to us.

—*Friedrich Nietzsche*

Tone is a slippery slope that many of us slip on and some of us choose to slide down on our asses. Others intentionally bury their heads in order to deny culpability. I have worked with junior groups, mixed groups, senior groups, under-sophisticated groups and slick productive groups. I really have. And I can tell you without a doubt that there is someone, at least one someone, who believes that another member of his or her group, is thoughtfully and deliberately malicious. Surprised? Yup, I am surprised each time too.

Ever find yourself in a disagreement or a full-out argument with someone and you say something like, "relax, chill-out, calm down or collect yourself"? These words can be said with great affection, subtle loathing or pure self-interest - all done in the same vein of making whatever is being said, about whatever topic to stop. Please stop.

And no matter how tactful the tone, no matter how saccharine, no matter how positive in its delivery, that will be a tone that will not override the dismissiveness of the words. Always, without exception. Have you ever been asked to calm down and responded by accepting the advice, sitting down in a lazy, wide-legged way, tilted back in the seat, taken a deep cleansing breathe and happily acquiesced, abandoning your original message altogether? "Thanks. Yes, I think I will relax, as you said. Ahhh. This is much better. What was I thinking earlier? What was I going on about? Ahhh." NO! You have never done this, you've never seen anyone take your advice to do the same, nor will you ever.

Tone is best practiced when the words you are speaking are complementary, not contradictory. You don't really mean relax. You mean something along the lines of, "You know that emotion your expressing right now? Well, to be totally honest with you it's darn inconvenient. How about we press pause and pick this up later? Say, around 3:00 this afternoon are you free then? Or better still, move ahead entirely as I have little to no interest in what you are going on about and just don't want to invest the energy in faking it any longer. Thanks so much."

Choose a positive tone that will take your conversations forward, not alter their path to parts unknown.

CHAPTER 40

ACKNOWLEDGEMENT

In every relationship, the work is never just in the positive actions we do for each other, but in the follow up.

—*Yehuda Berg*

I highly recommend that greetings and salutations be an integrated set of rituals in every professional's working life. Say hello when you first meet someone each day, no matter how many days, weeks, and years you've worked together. We actually don't notice when we greet each other; it is the omission of this courtesy that generally gets our ire up. The same is true of saying goodbye or good night at the end of your day. This acknowledgement is just as important when you are at the higher end of authority, perhaps even more so. It is a social grace that many of us cling to as examples of respectfulness. What's not to be gained then by saying hello?

I have worked in many unionized environments. The post-secondary schools in southern Ontario are all unionized, a fact that seems only to come to our collective consciousness when teaching assistants vote to strike and undergraduate classes get cancelled as a result. This can hit our pocketbooks very quickly and so we pay attention.

Yet there are actually many unions on each of these campuses. There are university-specific unions like YUSA (York University Staff Association) and better-known international unions such as Steelworkers and CUPE. I've worked with the University of Toronto, York University, Ryerson

University, OCAD University, University of Guelph, McMaster University and many community colleges, too.

Within soft skills workshops on each of these campuses, without fail, at some time over my twenty years of experience I've listened to frustrations and some disbelief at scenarios like "X" passing me in the hall and "looking right through me." Nothing, no acknowledgement of another human in the same space whatsoever. "Like I wasn't even there." Yet, we email, know each frequently, sit on the same committee, park our cars in the same lot, each bring the same kind of yoghurt that sits in the Department's fridge, etc.

I've also found myself working in many for-profit corporations (none of which am I at liberty to name). All of them are non-unionized environments. The ones at the top of my mind, as I write these words, are all in the US. I've worked in New York City, Charlotte, Tampa, Atlanta, and many smaller places. Excluding New York City, I've heard similar complaints about interpersonal under-acknowledgement. People looking for a smile and, minimal, but deliberate interaction. Sure it sounds somewhat different. Usually something like, "Sure he said hello, but he scowled at me. Nothing about my day, my work, my kids, my project, not even the weather." The want for acknowledgement is the same.

CHAPTER 41

NAMES: SPELLING VERSUS PRONUNCIATION

I call everyone 'Darling' because I can't remember their names.

—Zsa Zsa Gabor

One of the very first lessons I learned in being a successful group leader or facilitator in corporate settings is how significant people's names really are - they relish them. Take names seriously, respectfully and intentionally - your thoughtfulness will be appreciated.

There are some months when I may lead fifteen to twenty different groups of people in different companies, in a variety of industries and in several countries. What is true in each group, no matter who the members are? Each person wants to be recognized as a member of the group, and the only way we have of doing so equitably and legitimately is by both learning and using each other's names. I have learned that there is much tolerance for mispronunciations as long as there is effort. And, of course, a sincere effort is being made at getting the name right. We are quite forgiving of our names being poorly pronounced if there is an intention of truly, eventually getting it right. While, on the other side of this tolerance is brutal judgement, and even a trace of scorn and malice when we have our names misspelled, especially in an e-mail with a mass distribution. In this particular case, one misspelling can lead to a long-term, multi-person confusion, which often then also leads to the same name being mispronounced. There are clear implications to building one's brand if your brand has either been misnamed or renamed by unfortunate spelling. Brands can happen by accident or malice. They are designed with intention.

Learn people's names; make it your mission to correctly and often refer to others by name. Remember, as professionals we are all quite vain, myself included. We like to hear the sound of our own names. We like to see our names written by others. Use this to your advantage.

CHAPTER 42

PERSONAL REAL ESTATE

It's your space with or without tape on the floor.

Remember WKRP in Cincinnati? It was a great show. If you've never seen it it's definitely worth a few minutes of your time to check out the clips on YouTube. I personally recommend the scene of Venus teaching about the parts of an atom to a teenage gang member who is considering dropping out of high school. It is context-driven learning at its best; making each part of the atom relatable and meaningful to the student. But I digress ...

As for personal real estate, it's another WKRP character, Les Nessman (played by Richard Sanders) who I want to reference here. You see Les had the title of News Director and thought that as such he deserved an office. The station did not give him one, so Les placed thick yellow tape on the floor surrounding his desk, clearly indicating where walls and a door "should" be. Les is after his colleagues respecting his imaginary door and walls, simulating knocking and keeping the sanctity of the illusion of his own separate space alive throughout every conversation. Les is committed to his tape, albeit a bit extreme, and he has every intention of requiring others to abide by and live around his "office walls and doors." Privacy comes very expensively his way, if it comes his way at all.

Everyone has the right to some form of privacy on-the-job. I have a small example of courtesy about respecting the privacy of documents or any visible work on someone's desk. Eyes up please—whether it is a physical copy of a report or a soft copy of a partially completed e-mail on someone's monitor. I often recommend asking if there is anything that would be best turned over or if a screen might be better positioned out of sight during a conversation. You will be surprised at how delighted people are at your offering to be excluded from the possibility of prying into their privacy. This is an essentially simple and effective way of building your influence capital with others on-the-job. Try this out.

The other extreme is that people are occasionally so flattered by your offer to look away or to provide them a moment to collect their things that people start to share what can be privileged or private information with you. This has happened to me many times, and has always left me with a chuckle after the meeting because the genuine intention was for me to *not* be included into private matters. Yet because of my offer I have been brought into some loop that I may not have even known existed. It's just like speaking privately with Les in his "office," with the invisible door closed of course.

CHAPTER 43

WATCH YOUR BRAND

*Do not laugh at yourself. Instead, laugh with yourself. There
is a huge difference.*

Your brand is the combination of tangible and intangible characteristics
that make you unique. Branding is developing your specific image: with
an eye toward specific results in your relationships.

If you do not choose the specific language to describe your skills,
competencies, educational background, experience and overall
contributions, it will be chosen for you. It's as simple as that. Be active and
choose your brand or be branded. The next part of watching your brand is
in the absolute necessity of then repeating your specific chosen language.
Think of this as an advertising campaign or an educational blitz. Same
difference. When you educate those who you work with on the quality and
uniqueness of your work - that is your brand. When you allow others to
label and assign language describing your work that is your brand. Make
it; don't have it dished out to you.

Because if you don't brand yourself, others will for you. Promise.

Most professionals are not proactive in establishing and building a
career brand. You hope your actions speak for you when you are seeking
promotion or a new job. It is necessary to take the time to implement some
very basic marketing practices to help build a career brand and to make you

a more attractive professional: choose your language and repeat. Slogans for products, shoes or soft drinks, do exactly this.

Branding can be described as many things, but it's best defined as a promise of the value of the product that is better than all the competing products and that that promise will be delivered successfully. That is good branding not necessarily a good product, but as consumers we sure hope for the best. That is the result of good branding to win favour to your direction. See how it works?

Over the years, I have worked with more than a few outplacement career transition management and/or consulting firms. Brand is almost exclusively discussed only when a person is seeking employment and it can simply be too little, too late. Your brand is a day-to-day reality, an on-the-job personal challenge. Please don't wait until you are in career transition.

Here's one of my favourite branding stories, I call it "Sometimes my Brain just doesn't Work."

When my daughter was nine years old she suddenly and intensely decided that she wanted to have her nails done, her hair done, and have a facial. She became quietly obsessed with make-up and every other stereotypical interest that grown women are portrayed to have in the media. It was shocking to me. I don't remember going through a phase like it myself and until then, my daughter, Sarah, had not shown much, if any, interest in any of these female trappings. But it happened, and I supported her interests. During this phase I took Sarah to a girl-oriented salon/spa, all the same amenities and services of a regular salon with the added dimensions of sparkles, candies and a waiting room for parents. The girl clients are treated like royalty - wearing plush slippers, having their hair and nails done, as well as facials applied while the staff of very done-up adult women dote and coo over them. The girls are obviously new to the spa rituals and have to be guided from one service station to the next with kind gestures. The whole salon is clearly organized to be client-focused and pleasant on the senses; it smells sweet, it is decorated with pretty colours and an abundance of cute accessories, there is loud pop music playing, and the girls appear to really enjoy it.

I had plans of hanging out in the waiting room with the other listless parents and reading and writing (with noise-reduction ear buds in, of course). It was a win/win as far as I expected. Sarah would get all done up and I would get all caught up.

Before I made my way to the waiting area, I loitered around and took a few pictures of my young daughter in full spa mode, with a lovely smile on her face. She was having a good time. After she had donned the robe, she sat in a plush purple velour chair shaped like a high heel shoe, while eating gummy worms. The services began with a facial and a staff member, a young woman herself who may have been a University student by day, was mixing a facial concoction for Sarah. And while doing so loudly said, "Sometimes my brain just doesn't work" and stopped what she was doing. She said it again as she walked over to a counter to her left and dumped out the mixture before laughing uncomfortably to herself and turning back to Sarah with a grand swinging movement, all the while grinning. "My brain is just not here today!" She was chastising herself for an error and obviously starting over again. Round 2 with the facial ingredients. Not a big deal. Or is it? Sarah looked at me and rolled both her eyes back into her head and inhaled dramatically at the same time. Yes! If your client is a pre-teen girl who is disillusioned by your representation of your brand while in your care with a mouth full of candy - you have dropped the brand ball. How much more stacked in your favour could the cards have been? Sarah wanted a spa experience. All this young woman had to do was deliver one. Sarah did eventually have her facial. And she ate way too much candy all the while. Salon experience – done. Check.

It was a few weeks after the visit that Sarah and I could speak about the "silly" women who were at the salon. And how they really didn't "look or sound" like they knew what they were doing. Yeah, the brand had been clearly set for her. Even if you feel like your brain isn't working while on-the-job, fake it. Your brain will thank you, so will your brand.

This was an epic fail for the salon. An epic victory for down-to-earth women everywhere. Welcome Sarah to the fold. Life is better in sensible shoes (most of the time anyway).

COMPLIMENT PEOPLE TO OTHERS

Reverse reciprocity is behind the teenager's rebellion and the denied lovers' tenacity.

When you say good things about someone, the compliment usually makes its way back. There can be long, slow waves of reciprocity or quick bursts of activity. It's amazing really. Organizational Behaviour theories speculate about the spheres of influence that we each have in organizations. These theories often disregard the impact of the language we include in our conversations. After all, the unit of measurement of any organization's culture is the simple conversation. A lot of this book is dedicated to the celebration of the impact of one's choices in each and every conversation as building blocks of your professional success. Don't disregard that next conversation as an opportunity to (re)build.

We all like hearing that someone thinks well of us, especially when a third party is involved. By complimenting someone to others, there is a further validation to your comments that directly telling your compliments to someone first-hand just lacks. It's another dimension, an insinuated confidence in your comments as you are making them public.

Triangulating this process allows for a wider influence on behaviour.

Compliment in front of others, it's more important than one-on-one. Think public versus private.

Be sure to cc others in email. Spread the word. This is easy and really works to develop relational rapport.

The real value here (in addition to contributing to someone having a positive-charged day) is the opportunity to see how that same someone reacts to the compliment. This is soft skills manna from heaven. This is information that you can gather that you have no other way to access.

CHAPTER 45

SMILE OFTEN

A smile is a curve that sets everything straight.

—*Phyllis Diller*

A smile can be a bridge between colleagues and, better still, a way for your approach to the day that may be regarded as positive and optimistic. This one is actually much harder than it sounds as we all get so focused that it can be the first thoughtless absence in our communication, albeit non-malicious.

You've probably heard all those depressing statistics on how many times per day young children laugh versus adults (urban myths put children at outrageous daily laugh levels of anywhere from 300-750 while adults somewhere in the 15-25 range). I don't claim to know what the exact figures may be, but I do claim to know that kids laugh a heck of a lot more than adults. And I also comfortably claim that this isn't necessarily a hindrance to a high quality of experience. Some of the funniest people on the planet do not often laugh out loud at all. Are they miserable individuals? No. It is the subtle eyebrow raise, the corner of the mouth grin, the smirk tied to a quick exhale and the shrug-like forward shoulder roll of laughter that adults tend to offer much more readily than an outright guffaw. You don't see statistics comparing adult smirks to children's laughs now do you? Maybe there is a missed opportunity in sociological research here. (Maybe not.)

I'm not a proponent for the fake laugh. It's very hard to pull off without acting class and practice. We can intuit that it's fake. Easy as that.

I am a proponent, however, of the fake smile with the qualifier that you're smiling at/for/with yourself. The body can literally lead the mind on this. I dare you to feel miserable with a huge grin on your face.

I also smile to myself when I am walking down the hallway into a presentation too, in every venue or corporation I find myself in, and at the start of each professional coaching session I deliver. It works.

When you smile you are bringing positive messaging to your brain and demonstrative a positive perspective to the world.

COMMUNICATION FOR TOMORROW AS WELL AS TODAY

Everything you think is immutable is about to change.

The present is the location you can expand on with confidence in your communications. In the present tense you have the most personal autonomy to express. There is a certainty in the scale and scope of the present that is often under-appreciated. It is a squandered chance for you to demonstrate clearly your specific communication purpose and educate others as to how much mastery you wield in your role. The challenges and opportunities in the immediate situation (in that brief present that we each have) keep our own thoughts as well as the attention of your listener(s) in check. This is powerful stuff that can be leveraged to effectually persuade and influence others.

	Present Logical Most Available Control	
Past Emotional		**Future** Emotional
No Control		Some Control

Control & Influence

Keep the majority of your professional speaking and writing in the present tense. We can intuit that we each have the most available control and influence over ourselves, others, and processes at this moment - right here, this afternoon (or morning, depending on when you're reading this, of course) today, this week even. In contrast, speaking and writing of what has already happened, equally dilutes your authority, whether yesterday, last month, or last year, for that matter. Why? Because we know that the past happened. We also know the past is open to some subjectivity.

When your conversations and writing are present-tense-focused, you ingratiate yourself with much more ease. You are able to keep focus on your areas of control ultimately engendering more confidence. It is sometimes even inspirational, especially if you combine it with a business story or two. This is how to keep people engaged in conversation. This is how to have others reminded and informed of how your today (tactical) is directly linked to yesterday and tomorrow (strategic).

CHAPTER 47

THE VELCRO® EFFECT

I like dreams of the future better than the history of the past.

—*Thomas Jefferson*

Brief Disclaimer # 1: This is an idea that I honestly don't remember when I first heard of it - it has always been around much like its namesake fastener. I don't know if any one person has laid claim to this term. So that's me not being able to give due credit and at the same time not discrediting myself.

Less Brief Disclaimer # 2: I have recently become a fan of a spectacular BBC1 produced television show called 'Qi." It is a British staple on their local television with reruns running daily on another British station called Dave, in addition to weekly new episodes. It is smart television and worth watching. Check it out. It was on a recent episode of Qi that I learned that the manufacturers of Velcro® are convinced that there is no such thing as Velcro®. Apparently what most of us think of as Velcro® is indeed more accurately referred to as a 'hook and loop fastener'. Pretty sure the explanation has something to do with trademark names being appropriated into everyday language and not maintaining their distinction. Think: Kleenex in North America or Hoover in the UK. That sort of makes sense to me, but at the same time, it *is* Velcro®.

Take a few seconds here please and think about Velcro® and what it does. How have you used it? Where is it valuable in your daily life? It is a fastener that uses two tiny hooking surfaces that face opposing directions. When these two surfaces are attached, they form a strong connection that requires a strong pull to tear them apart. Velcro® also offers a rather satisfying "rip" sound if done in one continuous motion. Like any fastener, over time and/or with use, the two sides can lose some of their grip on the other, weakening their connection.

From this understanding of Velcro® (I'm pretty sure it does exist, by the way, but that's just me), we move to the Velcro® Effect. Think about any on-the-job scenario. There is the side that is "hooked" and the side that is a "hook." These two sides come together to create the scenario. The Velcro® Effect is how we can get hooked repeatedly over time by the same stimuli. Think about being reminded of a conflict each time you see that person's name in your email inbox. No matter what that new email is about, that conflict will pop up in your thinking when you see that name, won't it? That's an example of the Velcro® Effect in action. This is also called performance history in psychological circles; that past relationships or interactions will act like Velcro® and trigger the negative perceptions in the present.

Letting the past trigger your present and potentially influence your future is self-defeating. Rip the Velcro® apart. You'll be glad you did.

PART 4

PRESENTATIONS

CHAPTER 48

VISUALIZING AND MENTAL REHEARSAL

Visualize this thing that you want, see it, feel it, and believe in it. Make your mental blue print, and begin to build.

—*Robert Collier*

Your subconscious mind cannot differentiate between a real event and one that is vividly visualized. Visualizing has an effect on your brain's elasticity. A synapse is a pathway that is formed in your brain through repetition. So if you continually practice a task mentally or physically, that pathway strengthens. Your brain really can't tell the difference. This is an amazing opportunity to leverage in terms of your professional development.

So your brain actually changes shape in an attempt to help you get better at doing something. It changes shape! How amazing is that? This means if mentally repeating something makes you better at it, then repeated visualization will increase your performance.

There are many ways to prepare for a presentation, regardless of the technology you use. Any presentation training worth a moment of your time will recommend to you that you visualize your presentation *before* you deliver it. I recommend the day before, maybe even as you lay your head to rest for the night. Use your mind's eye to visualize your audience as best you can, and the space in which you will be presenting. Visualize from your perspective as the presenter - take a mental tour. If there are faces you know attending your presentation, imagine them there in the audience. If you are going before a group for the first time, visualize humans, any humans, but lots of them in the audience. If you are not sure what the space will be like, then visualize one that you like. Walk around the stage or podium.

Think about your presentation and how you will feel when you present. Try to visualize what your preferred feelings will be as you present successfully. Present your slides or deliver your talk as perfectly as you can in your visualization. No one can see you or hear you, so be perfect - whatever that means to you. And then, do it again. Visualizing is a great self-soother for nerves, an easy way to program our brain for success and a lovely skill to create the realities we want to experience in-person.

Sports professionals have been coached on the values of practicing visualization for decades. The mental rehearsal can improve the performance results. Athletes have long praised the value of physical and mental rehearsal. It's old news to them.

Michael Jordan scored more baskets in his mind than he ever did on the court. He didn't become one of the greatest athletes of the century with physical skill alone. It is well known that before every match, Jordan relaxed and visualized himself making basket after basket, in every imaginable scenario.

Picture your own success. Over time it will become a quick to-go thought exercise that you can pull-up in your mind when you need it. I practice this one – I really do. And it is a big part of practicing to present and being in front of a group, not to be perfect but to make the skills permanent.

BREATHING

Space is the breath of art.

—Frank Lloyd Wright

Visualize stress is leaving your body. Cleanse your thoughts. Refresh your depth of breath. Do it quickly. It can help. Honest.

I know it must sound commonsensical, but it is truly amazing how many of us hold our breath or breathe shallowly when we are uncomfortable. And we have already established that most of us are quite uncomfortable speaking/presenting before a group - any group for that matter.

In Tai Chi it is suggested that practitioners focus on movement and breath simultaneously; breathing so deeply and fluidly that the breath is filling the soles of one's feet with each inhalation and travelling up and through the whole length of the body with each exhalation. A tall order for some of us who are still trying to walk, breathe and occasionally chew gum at the same time.

I have worked with many skilled, experienced professionals who come to presenting, forget to breathe and cause their own presenting downfall. They start to flush with redness, they pant, they start to compensate with their bodies and move about awkwardly. I have witnessed more than one executive pant so wildly because of shallow breathing patterns that they were bouncing up and down about 10 cm with each inhale. Very distracting.

The first identifiable display of nervousness in any presenter is their breathing. It impacts voice, tone, inflection, volume and body language. Not to mention the distraction and toll on the body when it is being denied adequate oxygen. Breathing is an undercurrent or foundation on which you may create your own state of calm despite adrenalin pumping. Please don't take it for granted. Breathing (intentionally and purposefully while presenting) has saved more than one professional I have coached to collect their thoughts, focus their words and deliver a pristine presentation despite nerves, anxiety, limited preparation time, time constraints or unexpected technical issues (e.g. the projector just won't acknowledge your laptop no matter what the IT Department does.)

Breathe.

CHAPTER 50

APPEAL TO SELF-INTERESTS

You are your words; your words are you.

We are all vain. And putting humanity's vanity at the fore of your thinking will keep you in check. It will allow you to know both what your presentation's specific purpose is, and to ensure that you speak that purpose as close to the very start of your presentation as you can muster. Yes, give the "secret" away. This educates your audiences (no matter what size) on exactly what and how to be thinking as you proceed. This is a subtle and remarkably effective shift you can take in your thinking, preparation, and delivery. This one works well even when the presenter is obviously nervous. It is about your audience having set expectations that are then met. How satisfying is that? This satisfaction will buy you a generous amount of understanding and a bit of slack when it comes to your delivery. I have seen this work hundreds of times.

To effectively persuade someone, you need to understand what makes that person tick - just a little bit. This is much easier than it sounds. You need to know one item, just one item or area, if you will, of interest. Speak about it, and that person will expand upon the topic, contextualize it, explain it, and often give you top-of-mind examples. And most likely, in the process, they will reveal additional self-interests.

Self-interest is not synonymous with selfish. This is an important clarification. And an easy error that many professional make. But not you - at least not anymore.

Empathy is sometimes elusive, but always applicable. Putting yourself into the other's position - no matter who they are - is at the very core, the heart of this challenge. Most of us behave to satisfy and even validate our own self-interests. What is your audience's self-interest? Why are they listening to you? Why are they attending your presentation?

Don't assume that other people will do what you want merely because you're a credible person, or can articulate logical arguments. You also have to motivate people to action by showing them why it is in their best interests to do as you suggest to be the preferred route.

W.I.I.F.M. It stands for 'What's in it for me?' Many professionals use this acronym in many industries. This acronym works well in focusing the content and delivery of your presentations on the purpose first and then defining, highlighting and outlining the benefit(s) to your listener(s). Use it to jolt yourself into an other-orientation rather than focusing on yourself. Asking, "what's in it for me?" can push us out of our own heads and into the other person's or the group's interests.

These are the simplest and most provocative questions to use in guiding yourself to speak with a purpose that serves your listeners well:

What does my listener need to know and require from me?

How can I service my listener's purpose in listening to me in the first place?

How may I speak to their self-interest and vicariously service my own interest of communicating successfully?

EMBRACE PAUSE

The first problem for us all, men and women, is not to learn,
but to unlearn.

—*Gloria Steinem*

Embrace pause. This is one of my very favourite expressions. I use it when I teach presentation skills, supervisory skills, coaching, and many other topics. It is the most eloquent, gentle and clear way that I have found in my career, so far, to ask someone to kindly please "shut up."

It is the reality that your audience cannot process information in two forms at the same time. What does that mean? It means that when you reveal a slide in PowerPoint and *immediately* begin speaking about the contents of that slide, your audience is neither listening to you nor reading the data on your slide. They are in a state of imposed limbo that leads to distraction and ultimately disengagement - that's a presentation fail.

Sticking with PowerPoint, the best practice, and it comes very easily with a little practice, is to introduce your next slide *before* revealing the slide. How? Here's one of the best tricks you can use with all of your presentations, but with PowerPoint in particular. Press the letter "B" while in slideshow mode and the slide is blacked out. The screen goes dark, there is no progression to your slide deck, and you then have your audience looking at you, listening to you - that's a presentation success. Press the letter "B" a second time and the slide is revealed. This is also available to you using the letter "W" which will white out the screen and also not interact with your slide deck while in slide show mode. A second press of "W" and your slide returns unchanged. Although it keeps the beam of light from the projector on, so most of the time the letter B works best.

It can flow this way:

After letter "B" is pressed and there is a black screen, introduce the slide. "This next slide contains a great deal of information, what I'm going to ask you to do is specifically focus on the third column from the left, the one in blue. You'll see that column is going to be how you can best understand how we have made progress from Q1 to Q3 of this fiscal year." Now reveal the slide with a second letter "B" and embrace pause. Stop talking. Stand there. Smile. Look engaged. Breathe. Control your thoughts and actions. It may feel like an eternity, but it is really a handful of seconds. And in those few seconds, your audience will do as you recommended, they will be looking at the blue third column from the left. Audiences are remarkably obedient and appreciate clear, easy to follow instructions.

You will know when those few seconds have passed; it may vary from slide to slide, from audience to audience. But each time you will know when to start speaking; your embrace of pause is over because your audience will look back at you. People usually will spend approximately 5-8 seconds reading a slide, no matter how dense with data and tables or sparse with pictures the slide may be. After which they will all redirect their collective gaze on the presenter as a cue to continue.

Get comfortable with silence.

CHAPTER 52

ASK QUESTIONS

Treat every conversation as a chance to make a first impression.

Questions move conversations forward. Answers can stall us. High-quality questions yield higher quality answers; hence less drag to the overall conversation's momentum. Low-quality questions inevitable yield low, and infrequently, very low to totally unconnected or misguided quality of answers; hence the challenge is to ask thoughtful questions. Most of us, most of the time ask poor quality questions. It's true.

Most of the time we don't spend even a nanosecond of time of the 0.5 calories of energy to think about a question *before* we open our mouths. I have this happen routinely when I am leading groups, especially around presentations skills. It is a self-soothing measure to speak in a group and to take that group on the journey of your thought processes that may or may not conclude with a question. That is my personal favourite, when an attendee asks for my attention and has the floor, then says something like 'I have a question,' and then rambles on for a bit about this or that (sometimes relevant sometimes not it really is of little consequence). And then this person will stop speaking without asking me a darn thing! There is nothing for me to respond to, nothing at all. So, like all professional presenters, I check-for-understanding by asking what I hope to be relevant questions in order to get that same person to that original question that sparked them to speak in the first place. It's just a matter of getting them to where their own thoughts were going.

Questions are much easier to answer if they are a) spoken aloud in a group setting, and b) formulated into the inquisitive version of the language (otherwise known as a question).

Larry King was often lauded during his career for the quality of his questions. I remember reading an article many years ago, which explained some of his success as an interviewer as predicated on his question-generating methodology. His approach included under-researching his interviewee (certainly much less so than the conventions of journalism) and to ask the questions that a layperson or fan would ask, rather than a professional journalist/broadcaster. It resulted in some questions that made Larry appear under-informed (how could he not when he intentionally under-researched?) and at other times remarkably insightful into the very aspects of his interviewee that had been overlooked or misunderstood in previous interviews: all because of the questions. No matter what the answers were.

Think first about what it is *exactly* that you are interested to know. And if you are uncomfortable asking the question, it is without a doubt the question you clearly *want* to ask. Am I suggesting that it is the correct question? No. Am I suggesting it is the incorrect question? Certainly not. I am telling you that your discomfort, that emotional information that you must tap into (intrapersonal knowledge) is a clear indicator of the significance of the information you seek from that other person (interpersonal knowledge). Don't hide behind it, celebrate it, think and then ask the question.

CHAPTER 53

BE WITH YOUR GROUP, FOR YOUR GROUP AND BECAUSE OF YOUR GROUP

If your worst fear is exposed, your worst fear becomes your enemy's best friend.

—*Jonah Kawarsky*

You are the presentation. You bring the value, the meaning, and the reason that there is a presentation at all. You. It is not a presentation because of the meeting, the data or because someone with more authority than yourself declared it was a good idea or requested (demanded) one. *You* are the presentation. Remember this.

Your group is keen to have their time well spent. This means that they want you to do a good job, in fact, a great job. Your group wants you to be well spoken, clear and have a message that is of value to them—each and every one of them.

All this can be easily summed up with some of the best advice I offer my groups: deliver information that speaks to them—of them, for them, and by them. And if you go into the process from the very starting point of how you think about the presentation or when you're creating your slide deck as if there is a divide between yourself and your audience, Stop! Regroup and start again. It is a shared experience and so make it a shared experience, not you alienating yourself, but instead aligning yourself.

You must necessarily find point(s) of connection, to be on the same side and support each other in a mutually beneficial experience. If you offer one piece of information that is contradictory to the group you cause an unnecessary rift that most presenters are just not well practiced enough to mend. Don't go there. Under-skilled presenters I have worked with often make the judgment error of over-exposure. If you had limited time to prepare, feel unsure of your content, have a tummy ache or feel like running from that boardroom screaming: do not offer these insights to your group - ever. Your group is there for the presentation to be of quality not to have it qualified or explained away as any less.

Revealing too much of yourself to your group is a risk to be taken very cautiously. Divisiveness can seriously erode your credibility this time, and decay your brand over time. Avoid any confessional tones and always be sincere. Exposing challenges does not necessarily validate your humanity as much as your inefficiency. Groups can tell the difference.

Remember we can be brutally judgmental if armed with information on which to make negative assumptions and/or conclusions. This is within your control to avoid as a skilled presenter.

CHAPTER 54

WORKPLACE DRIVE-BY

No one is so brave that he is not disturbed by something unexpected.

—*Julius Caesar*

Ever been the victim of what I affectionately call the "workplace drive-by"? It usually sounds something like this, "Diana, you know what would be really great? It would be great if you could just whip up our chat into a few PowerPoint slides, summarizing the key points, then shoot it over to me by email before the end of the day? Thanks." This is, of course, all being said rather quickly and somewhat sternly, by someone who has more authority than I do and is walking (trotting?) without so much as a pause let alone a breath as they continue to walk down the corridor past me and out of my sights altogether. Leaving me in their wake thinking a few choice words, but in addition to those, I'm also thinking, "Ahhh, what am I writing exactly? How many slides? Who is going to attend? Am I presenting? What just happened? I really wasn't listening in the first place, now what do I do? Argh."

Have you been a workplace drive-by victim?

There is help. But you've got to help yourself. Go ahead, prepare those slides with a *huge* watermark of "DRAFT" on each and every one (use the Master slide option) and send it along to the requester with a message that says something about the slides being a draft and ask if they are inline with their (mostly unspoken) expectations. The overwhelming majority of the time this has worked for me. You'll get a response that the slides you put together are "good enough" and that they will run with it from there. By the way, this is code for, "I'm not really too sure what the purpose is and I would rather not risk embarrassment. So I will do this myself." Now that's a win/win.

The drive-by does have a positive connotation that is worth mentioning here. You were asked because you have something to offer. Yes, on occasion it is that you happen to be the most convenient person to ask. Hands-down that is true. But, there are other times, maybe even most of the time, when you are asked because you have a perspective or an insight into that topic that will make assigning the task to you a recognition of sorts. Think about it.

CHAPTER 55

PURPOSE CLARIFICATION

Your strength of presentation delivery is what matters, not your introversion or extroversion.

Purpose. Purpose. Purpose. The most persuasive presenters are those who know why they are speaking. Doesn't that sound easy? Well, it's not always.

Purpose clarity may feel "obvious," like a "duh." I hear this feedback very frequently from clients. The group "knows" I'm presenting. They "know" why I'm here. Come on it's the monthly sales meeting, just like last month, just like there will be next month. The purpose is the same as last time, and the same as it will be next time. It's the same *every* time. Come on. This is a waste of time. Well, I have the privilege to tell you that they may indeed "know." You're right. But they absolutely require a reminder of your specific purpose each and every time. Why? Because, like you, your group has many other responsibilities, each one pushing and pulling them each workday. They need a reminder to focus, be in the present moment with you, and stay true to your presentation as an experience. So, not only is it a best practice for you to focus on your purpose: tell it to yourself before you start your preparation and but also tell it clearly to your group at the start of speaking. Ask yourself, what is the purpose of my presentation? The specific purpose? It is understandable that so many of us leave presentations thinking, "So what?" and "What was that all about?" It's all about purpose clarification.

Now it is your obligation as a skilled presenter to back that purpose up as well as you can. The easiest way to do so is with data - pick the data to support the purpose, and then build your thoughts and ultimately your words on this sturdy foundation. Keep in mind data alone is flat. It is the value of the data to your audience that the skilled presenter will emphasize; including emotional appeals.

This really is about you explaining *why* what you are speaking about is important. Building your case, or telling your story is an important differentiator when it comes to presenting well. Few of the professionals I work with have focused on this prior to working with me and everyone tells me that this is a huge benefit. While speaking in front of a group, it is not enough to be the "boss" or the subject matter expert. Although that can sure be a great start. It isn't necessarily how one is necessarily going to be taken seriously. How to be taken seriously comes in how you build your rapport and reinforce your credibility as a presenter through the supporting data or evidence you include in your content. Stick to your purpose – every time.

CHAPTER 56

USE EMOTIONAL APPEALS

Emotional does not mean emotive.

Presentations of the most technical or specific topic need to appeal to the emotions just as much (perhaps even more so) than non-technical or general topics. I remember working with the internal audit team of a multi-national pharmaceutical company over a decade ago. It was in their suburban Montreal offices. An internal audit team is a vital part of every organization. Despite this the rest of every organization avoids internal audit similarly to how I avoid doing Excel Spread sheets whenever and by whatever means possible. (Not where I excel at all. Haha.) Why do we avoid this very important group? Well, who welcomes the unsolicited call or email from internal audit? No one waits to receive that call or open that email. Internal audit doesn't call to let you know how well you are in compliance with the current policy or regulation, now do they? They call to correct, clarify, confirm and make your work verifiable.

This particular internal audit team I am remembering had prepared a PowerPoint slide deck for an important annual meeting that was chockfull of complicated graphs, copied and pasted verbatim government-issued policies, calculations, financial models and risk assessment summaries; lots of vital data. The whole deck could have been sent with a brief explanatory cover email and would have been a heck of a lot more successful than as it was as a presentation. When I asked what value the presenters were bringing to the presentation itself, there were Quebecois crickets chirping - loudly might I add. Silence filled the room. It was awkward. A total disconnect.

What did that mean? The team had to stop and think about what the point really was of going through the exercise of presenting the data. They had always presented this data. Did it have to be presented? Could it be replaced with an email? No, was the conclusion. It was important o explain how they had ascertained certain figures and how other figures were comparable to the previous yeas as well as the opportunity to forecast to the next. Ahhh! That was much closer to the purpose. Whew! The team was, at first, shocked and then quickly relieved. And they pulled together a killer slide deck with a purpose that had emotional appeals woven throughout the fabric of their data-driven slide deck.

Their numbers were clear and correct. Of course, we all want to work with internal audit; after all it is a vital function. The more seamless our relationship with them is well the better, because that means we can continue doing our own work, have internal audit validate and verify (which is their work) and the organization as a whole moves forward smoothly. Without knowing the value of internal audit's data, it is that much more difficult to answer their next call or reply to their next email, despite each of us knowing how important their work really is in the larger scope of continuous improvement.

If you and your presentation can be replaced by an email, please do so. I thank you. Your team thanks you. We all thank you.

Emotional appeals are the means by which we connect the data to our audiences; where meaning is manufactured and data is contextualized as significant. In other words, please focus on bringing value by applying your information to everyone's business interests. That's how everyone contributes to mutual business success.

The WIIFM (remember the What's In It For Me?) of your presentation will inevitably include data *and* emotionality. And if it does not initially, try to empathize with your audience—their fears, frustrations, interests, and uniqueness. In extreme forms, think about the TV Evangelists of the late 1980s and early 1990s - no matter what you may think about their message, they were definitely connecting emotionally with their audiences.

Now emotional does not mean that you are forfeiting logic. On the contrary, your emotional appeals compound, support, demonstrate, contextualize, and showcase the logical data. There is room for you to create an emotional connection with your audience no matter what the specific content of your presentation. This is how you make your data come alive.

HUMOUR SEPARATES THE MEDIOCRE FROM THE PRETTY DARN GOOD PRESENTER

I have one husband, one son, one daughter, one cat and one mortgage. One is more than enough husband. I am way too old for more children. The cat stays mostly to herself and if anyone wants my mortgage - it's yours.

It has long been a standing piece of effective business presentation advice to incorporate some humour into one's presenting materials or presenting style. This is not news to you or to me. Humour is impactful. Humour is how we tend to position information, package information, deliver information and hold onto information all in one solid swing. It is a great skill. Some of the funniest people I know have no idea why they are funny. This usually only adds to their humour. Funny, huh? My daughter, Sarah, was born funny. So much so when she was all of 2 she would often make an off-hand comment or observation that would crack up the room. She would immediately bursts into tears because everyone got her jokes but her. That just made the jokes even funnier.

It is often suggested that the "safest" humour is a joke about one's self. This is actually not exactly true. So please be cautious. Remember that we are looking for you to be a credible presenter. And all too often an under-skilled presenter will crack a joke about himself or herself only to undermine their status and alienate themselves from their audience. There is no redemption once you've done this. It is an epic presentation fail.

It is the ability to laugh *with* yourself and not *at* yourself that is the successful choice here. When you put yourself down, even mildly diminish your work's value or just suggest that you are not accurate, correct, or verifiable in your results, you give others the green light, a tacit permission slip, to do the same. And so we are quite obliging to think less of you and treat your work accordingly.

And while I am a fan of any group sharing a brief moment of reflection or even separation from content in order to re-fuel the collective attention span, such humour must not diminish or in any way tarnish the credibility of the presenter. Watch your brand and remember that any subtraction or distraction from your brand has a professional can be very difficult if not impossible to recoup.

PART 5

PERSUASION & INFLUENCE

CHAPTER 58

FRAMING

Conduct your own gap analysis on your use of language and space.

Framing is a communication technique, which is often misunderstood and seldom appreciated for its potential impact on your overall persuasiveness. Framing often can come to mind when we find ourselves in an emotionally heightened state, usually when engaged in a debate (argument?) with others whom we care about. When you choose to refer to that in-law of yours by their role and specific connection to your partner/spouse (for example "your mother or your sister") versus by that person's first name, you are framing your subsequent comments in marginally negative, and substantially passive-aggressive terms. There are a variety of negative connotations that are both inferred and evoked just by framing that relationship as further distant from yourself and by insinuation your perspective in that immediate conversation (argument?)

Yes, framing is as simple as a chosen turn of phrase or choice of words (please think back to the branding advice I shared with you earlier) it is integral to your overall professional influence to use it to bring your listeners to a perspective or shared meaning. On-the-job framing can accentuate your allegiance to a specific individual, team or concept as well as intentionally create distance to separate or suggest a disassociation.

That under-skilled colleague of yours who is chairing a meeting and suggests that the question posed by another colleague is a "good" question before answering it is framing his or her response and offering a verbal nod of appreciation to the asker. And when a different colleague asks another question of the same Chairperson, that question is answered without it being offered any label at all, let alone "good." The asker notices. The whole group notices. And the relationship is now affected in a negative manner as a result. Avoidable. Simply avoidable. Think about framing. It is a simple and high impact communication skill to master.

Do not underestimate the undeclared authority and pronounced power of framing. It can be used for good as well as evil no matter what sort of mother-in-law or sister-in-law you may have. Framing influences your relationship each and every time you introduce it in each and every one of your conversations.

Here is a list of 4 Words and Phrases that you can use to frame in your conversations:

Thank You.

We love being thanked. It is an easy way to connect and reconnect. It is more than being polite.

Let me think about it and get back to you by____?

We love having the impression that we are being taken seriously and that you are thoughtfully preparing to engage with us. Be sure to set a firm time to follow-up and then do so. It does not mean you have a solution.

What else can you tell me about___?

We love having the opportunity to expand, especially if you have framed your interest in a positive manner. This phrase can have people doing double or triple takes.

How may I help right now?

We love having the offer made of going to or staying in the present tense through framing the conversation as immediately relevant. Keep it in the moment. Others will follow willingly.

CHAPTER 59

PROCESS OF YOUR PROGRESS

Your process is the progress.

Where are you right now in your career? In your overall maturation and development? In your industry? In the current role(s) you hold? Where are you doing what you do? Where else could you be doing that? Are you doing what you want to be doing? Why? Why not? Take a snap shot of your current reality. Now try to refocus on what future you would prefer. The conceptualization of your future is an important step in influencing your attainment of that same future. Intentionally engage in this thinking, considering possible actions you may take and/or relationships to create or dismantle will propel you in the direction(s) you seek. This is how you can self-advocate to create your future rather than have it happen to you. It is an active re-orientation to the passive unfolding that life offers each of us. We live passively unless we actively self-engage.

This is a simplified model to frame how you might think about your own professional development over time. Reading this little book may well be a part of your journey. Thank you. And congratulations too.

There are 5 Dimensions briefly explained for you to use as benchmarks of the process of your progress.

Give this a drop of consideration. It will be worth your time.

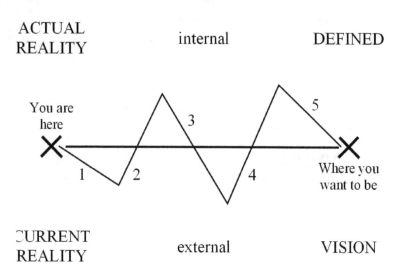

ACTUAL REALITY   internal   DEFINED

You are here

Where you want to be

CURRENT REALITY   external   VISION

Current Reality & Vision

5 Dimensions:

1. Reflective Action: Thinking about what you do, why you do it and ensuring it is linked to goals and objectives.
2. Vision: A clear future picture that informs the way effort is directed.
3. Self-Awareness: A realistic understanding of who you are; accurate reading of your emotions and their impact; accurate assessment of your strengths, limits and how others see you; a sound sense of your self-worth and capabilities.
4. Self-Management: Keeping disruptive emotions and impulses under control; adapting to changing situations; seeing the upside in events; drive to improve performance.
5. Authentic Engagement: Bringing who you are to your work. Internally directed, other-focused and open.

CHAPTER 60

THREE STEPS TO SELF-TALK AWARENESS

Your thoughts are your reality.

Self-talk awareness doesn't require any special equipment and it doesn't cost anything. All that is required is the willingness to stop and listen to our inner mental chatter with new or, at least, deliberate awareness.

Usually unchecked self-talk can easily fall into the rut of our past thinking patterns about our life choices and ourselves. Changing or re-directing this inner dialogue offers a chance at being more positive-focused and self-affirming. Remember that your self-talk has to only make sense to you. And you alone. That is actually the biggest challenge, because creating an awareness of your self-talk requires that you are first, conscious of what the heck you choose to think about, second, that you recognize you have choice and lastly that you are either pleased with it as it is or want to change it. There are benefits to be reaped at each of these stages, so don't sell yourself short and try to make it make sense to you for you and by you.

Another positive aspect of self-talk is that we can use it no matter how busy we are because it can be practiced and honed independent of our environment or in and of itself. It is portable, customized to fit you and ever available. Your self-talk is one of the most powerful tools for your overall self-management; it is often referred to as a form of active, in-the-world meditation.

Here are three straightforward steps to developing your Self-Talk Awareness:

Step 1: Observe your Self-Talk

Spend a moment in your head. What do you think about what you think about? Have you thought about this? Thinking about one's thinking is not a luxury reserved for philosophers. It is a fundamental activity that contributes to you grooming yourself, priming yourself for success.

Some key questions to consider: "What am I listening to?" or "What am I saying to myself?"

Step 2: Evaluate your Self-Talk

What you choose to think about and how you choose to think about those same topics are two sides of the same coin. The choice to delete, limit, amplify or multiply certain thoughts is the starting point for you to master your self-talk skills. What you choose to tell yourself leads to the language you assign to your thoughts, how you choose to share that language with others and in the final analysis really how you choose to define you world. It's a small way to be connected with your own world-view. Narratives are an important way of learning about how many of us choose to make sense of our lives and the world around us. Most organized religions offer compelling narratives, full of archetypal figures and even mantras (i.e. prayers?) to keep our self-talk in focus.

A key question to consider: "What am I telling myself about___?"

Step 3: Choose Positive over Negative Self-Talk

The subconscious mind is how we can influence our expectations within our conscious minds. Perhaps thinking about your own thinking can be best positioned as a bridge between the two that you can build out of sticks or cement. You can choose the materials.

A key question to consider: "What would I rather be hearing right now?"

CHAPTER 61

THE 180° TECHNIQUE

Shape the mind, not the body.

—*Sarah Kawarsky*

Disclaimer: I have known about this technique for nearly thirty years. I think it may be one of the concepts that resonated with me when I first learned about and eventually got certified in Life Skills Coaching in the early 1990s. That is as close as I can honestly come to a credit.

The 180° Technique simply takes the negative self-talk and turns it around 180 degrees. That does not mean that it is simply lived because for many of us we have spent a long time and a lot of effort telling ourselves the negative. The positive can feel remarkably foreign and even just plain ol' "wrong" in your own head.

In my work over the years in coaching people on a variety of challenges, professional growth is often best approached by starting at the thinking level with clients. Asking people to share their thinking is such an act of trust that it can be a while before people are willing to do so. It is amazing that we often have populated our own thoughts with commentary or observations that we will "say" to ourselves but know that it is ridiculous, wrong or anti-social to speak aloud. It is a good instinct to listen to. If your thoughts are of such a negative nature that sharing them reveals your otherwise unknown predispositions in relationships, stop and check your self-talk – now!

We often gauge intimacy in our relationship through the sharing of self- talk.

This is not a one-off technique. It is important to check-in regularly with your self-talk. Yes, I admit it. I have a reminder to do exactly this in my Outlook Calendar. It's every three months or so; a timeframe that works for me. Try it out for yourself.

CHAPTER 62

MIRRORING

Posture placement not posturing placement.

Mirroring is choosing to intentionally mimic someone's movements and/or posture. You will persuade them with your silent attention and influence how they speak at the same time. Unquestionably, it is a copycat technique that tends to stroke egos as it suggests that how you are holding yourself is the "correct" way to do so, so much so that I will follow in kind. This is important to remember because it is how you leverage body language to boost your own esteem and that of your partner. These boosts are silent validation of the relationship and your dedication to it being successful. Powerful stuff really.

Caution:

Do not mirror the behaviours of someone who is two or more layers of authority above you in your organization. I see this mistake all of the time. And, with the greatest frequency in professional firms e.g. legal or management consulting. In these firms I have observed many times that the managing partners and senior-level decision makers have a specific way of behaving. And that way may not be optimal, preferred, sanctioned or even acknowledged. It is however, ubiquitous and often obvious behaviour that can be very attractive to new Associates. It is these same new-ish staff members who aspire to be partners one day (soon?) who mistakenly mirror these senior behaviours and postures. And what a shock it is to those new Associates when they are sat down and offered some pretty negative (sometimes career-altering) feedback. They are told that they are "inappropriate, too eager, not professional and lack polish." It is usually those same mirroring skills that served these young lawyers so well throughout law school. Faculty are well known for enjoying being mirrored by their students; it's an ego stroke. So, yes most of them are genuinely shocked at this feedback.

I have had the pleasure of working with more than a handful of law firms and whenever I am called it is almost assuredly about a new Associate who other than some "unfortunate" choices when he or she had lunch with one of the managing partners has otherwise been labeled as a "High Potential." In other words, this term refers to a young lawyer who the firm sees with a profit-generating future. It is mirroring at its most dangerous in these situations. You see that High Potential lawyer usually wants to be a managing partner or at least wants more authority. And so it does make logical sense that presenting one's self as the managing partners do would be how to demonstrate one's latent destiny. Not true. It alienates the managing partner, it also showcases the High Potential's inexperience (I've heard the phrase "too big for her or his britches" often thrown about – believe it or not) and places the road to more authority and high profits for everyone on a much more circuitous path.

When I do come in and coach these High Potential lawyers and explain how this all works, it is gratifying to see how quickly the light bulb flicks on. They get it; they want to be successful. They re-adjust and use mirroring to their advantage from that point forward.

Do mirror colleagues or those in your organization who are one layer of authority your senior. This is the location where your choices of soft skills application and connecting with another human have the biggest potential for pay-off. Concentrate your efforts here.

There is a broad-brushstroke of possibilities when mirroring: almost infinite possible combinations and permutations to consider. The more obvious include hand gestures, leaning to one side and how one positions one's body on a piece of furniture (e.g. seated slouched or with a tall back). A great deal of social science can be seen to celebrate how we mimic each other unconsciously; aligning ourselves with others (validate group membership - sometimes called herd mentality) or physically distinguishing or differentiating ourselves from others (suggesting group leadership interests or aspirations – sometimes wrongly called management).

I am asking you here (challenging you really) to try out consciously mimicking by paying attention to others and following suit. It's worth the social experiment. Try it out.

CHAPTER 63

THE LEAN-IN TECHNIQUE

Empower yourself by being aware of the forces around you.

Disclaimer:

I am pretty sure that this one I can take total credit for. I put it together when I was first working on a keynote speech years ago for a women-only conference. I wanted to give a specific example of how to use one's body to complement or compound their words when at a meeting. How to help women professionals to make the most of meetings was the theme of my speech and it is a topic I have spoken to and taught in different formats many times since. This technique is not particular to women, but it is particular to ensuring you are leveraging the physical cues of another person who has more authority than you do in a specific situation.

The Lean-in Technique is a particularly effective mirroring technique; and please know that I both teach and practice this one. I have groups of professionals practice leaning in during seated conversations repeatedly as a means of bringing consciousness to one's body language and of expressing a silent commitment to their listener. The name is literal, when in a conversation, or listening to a colleague during a meeting, lean in towards that person while they are talking, adjust yourself if seated to face them as squarely as possible, you may even crane your neck a bit depending on the table height, seating arrangement and the number of attendees. While standing, lean-in towards the speaker from the waist up, slightly hunching your shoulders toward them with a subtle roll.

Try this. You will see that speaker's eyes widen, they will slow down their pace, and they will noticeably lean in towards you in reciprocation. Success!

SCARCITY

Life is short; economize your actions to govern your time.

Scarcity is a classic sales tactic to infuse urgency into any sales cycle. It offers the potential buyer a covert incentive in moving the relationship forward. Think of that 'Limited Time Offer.' 'This offer may expire without notice.' 'Valid only until the end of the business day – today.' You have heard and read this kind of stuff, we all have. Creating a sense of (false?) urgency and evoking emotion is the 1-2 punch of scarcity. It is especially attractive to advertising and sales professionals, perhaps much more so than to their consumers. It is also rather attractive to under-skilled managers who are trying to inspire their staff to share in their own want for speed. Scarcity inspires rushed decision-making and insinuates popularity or a high(er) demand. This is powerful persuasion in action; it influences you to make assumptions and to act on them – right or wrong.

Here's an illustrative story:

A childhood of scarcity versus a childhood of abundance.

When I was growing up, affection was a scarcity. So much so that demand was also influenced. There was little demand for affection from me in response to rarely being offered affection. None of this is of consequence to you or me until thirty or so years later. That was when my husband brought my frugality of offering affection to our young son, Jonah, to my attention, who knew?

Jonah and I were seated on our living room sofa watching a cartoon together. Sheldon, my husband, popped his head around the corner to have a parents-only exchange. Jonah must have been no more than two years old at the time, so we still had some private parent-only conversations. Sheldon scrunched up his face and motioned for me to move over on the sofa, closer to Jonah. So, I did. He then said something like, "You know you can hug him or hold his hand or something while you're there, it would okay." The penny dropped, the light bulb switched on. Yeah, of course. That *is* a great idea. I will now hug my son, I thought, and immediately shimmied over to be closer to him with my arm around his shoulders. I remember having these almost robotic thoughts to Sheldon's words. He was totally right. I knew he was. But it had honestly not dawned on me to be affectionate at that moment. I was just happy to be in a parallel position on the sofa. No more, no less. I squeezed up beside Jonah, and we hugged and cuddled for the remainder of the show. It was awesome and one of my favourite learning moments about myself as a new-ish parent.

Scarcity can be a contagion that makes abundance difficult to recognize. When you and your colleagues are always working under-the gun, under arduous and barely surmountable odds, with limited or reduced resources it can be ridiculously difficult see where or when you have opportunity to celebrate where there may be a little extra. Scarcity is a mind-set that erodes our appreciation of the present by clinging to an uncomfortable past or forecasting a gloomy future. It isn't always as simple as a hug, but it can be. I have shared that example of me having to be reminded to be affectionate many times over the years and it has been one of my most controversial stories. Who knew? Certainly not me. It shocks some that I didn't just "know" how to do this (You didn't hug your child?) and it confuses others who assume that I am obediently following my husband (You did what you were told?) Yes and yes are my answers. Both Jonah and I needed Sheldon to get our affection quotient from the red and into the black. Now Jonah had a much better shot at a childhood of affection abundance.

CHAPTER 65

TIMING

Everybody I know who is funny, it's in them. You can teach timing, or some people are able to tell a joke, though I don't like to tell jokes. But I think you have to be born with a sense of humor and a sense of timing.

—Carol Burnett

Know your group. Know your team. Know the cycles of your organization. Study the cycles of your own work and those of your colleagues.

That innovative idea to recreate the workflow process for one of the fiscal year-end responsibilities you happen to share with several of your immediate colleagues is *not* nearly as innovative if you share it and speak about it whilst in the drama and thick of meeting that same fiscal year-end responsibility. Timing is communication code for pacing yourself to supplement and support the circumstances (including your colleagues) of your work. That same innovative idea may prove more popular and ultra-innovative if you share it at the start of the new fiscal year. Once we have an idea or comment that comes to top of mind many of us can sincerely struggle to not blurt it out. Some of us admit to it feeling like it happens to us and the words have a life of their own. No, they don't.

Timing can make more of an impact than the idea itself. Choose your timing don't let it choose you.

CHAPTER 66

CONGRUENCE

A bad beginning makes a bad ending.

—English Proverb

Having our actions not only support, but to also lead to new, shared actions is the nugget of wisdom behind the concept of congruence. Sales people have long used congruence to get that deal. There is one car salesman who comes to mind who works at a local car dealership where my husband and I have bought several cars over the past decade or so. This fellow without fail will reach out intentionally towards myself or my husband. He predictably then gestures for one of our hands with his opened hand extended forward. Once he has one he grabs a light hold and shakes it simultaneous to the conversation continuing. While the negotiation of preferred terms continues, and how everyone can agree to potentially moving forward is still being actively discussed, all the while shaking hands. We continue the conversation to get the point where we are closing that deal. We keep talking, and we keep shaking hands. It may be important to include here that we have bought three cars from this same salesman. Go figure.

Congruence means you are setting people up to act, as you would prefer *before* their words catch up. It also means that you are stacking the deck in your favour that the words that you want to hear to corroborate that handshake are coming along any second now. Think about walking from your office to a meeting room with one of your colleagues. While still speaking and walking, if you begin to walk towards your preferred destination you have established an immediate subconscious connection with that colleague. Suddenly, you'll both be where it is you wanted to go before either of you have spoken a word about it. Congruence is the reason behind our creating mental links between specific actions and words. Talking with you leads me to specific spaces. Shaking hands means that we are in some form of agreement.

Congruence is often used by individuals who are afforded more authority in specific scenarios e.g. a Police Officer will guide you to slow down your driving without looking you in the eye or even looking in your direction, if there is a gesture of waving a hand slowly upwards and downwards offered in your direction. It works well whether or not you have blatant authority. Congruence is the skill you exercise to carve out overt authority for yourself regardless of everyone's role or the circumstance. It is how you can influence when you may be the unlikely influencer; think about that car salesman. We keep buying cars from him, don't we?

Think about how your gestures and interactions with others either support or detract from your message. Congruence is subtle and powerful. Try it out. Watch others.

USE RE-ENFORCEMENT

It's the repetition of affirmations that leads to belief. And once that belief becomes a deep conviction, things begin to happen.

—Muhammad Ali

Think about memorable people whom you have worked with over the years. I will bet that may of them outline, explain, and then summarize important points when they speak. In other words, tell them what you're going to tell them, tell them and then tell them what you've told them.

When I'm leading groups, it is a conscious technique that I take on to speak the same message several times if it is connected to my purpose. If it is in conversation, I know that the credibility of my purpose is reinforced when I can articulate the same message in a few ways.

Synonyms are your friend.

I can remember the moment in Grade 3, when I was only eight years old, and I figured out that a thesaurus was not a kind of dinosaur but instead a writing resource that if used properly not only impressed my teacher, it kept the teacher at bay. Yes! It is your vocabulary that will allow you to choose the language to, of course, establish and then reinforce your purpose.

When teaching I will often provide instructions with words such as, "Your task now is to choose or select. You are now going to pick …" By the time I get to pick, (the third synonym for the same action, the group has realized that there is an action I am about to tax/challenge them with and have perked up considerably – noticeably so every single time.

There is a lot of value to be found in repetition of key messages. Demonstrating that you can come at your message using a variety of language serves to build your brand as consistent and reliable.

CHAPTER 68

"OWN" YOUR MESSAGE

Don't sit and complain, stand and compliment.

—*Sarah Kawarsky*

Recognize that your message comes from your point of view, your beliefs of right and wrong, and your perceptions of good and bad. The use of personalized "I" statements such as, "I don't agree with you" as opposed to "You're wrong," allow you to take responsibility for and ownership of your message without suggesting that someone else is wrong or bad. We foster our perspective in part through our experiences and how we have chosen to make sense of them. The words we choose then reflect these assumptions. You have a clearer ownership when you can understand and better still identify where your perceptions originate.

Statements that judge others negatively can only foster resentment and resistance rather than understanding and cooperation.

Owning the message means that you are aware of the possible social risks that you are engaging in within that specific conversation, within that specific relationship. Some of us come to this form of social risk quite naturally and choose to withhold our opinions rather than share them until the "time is right." Others are convinced that there is no "right time" and so they are not convinced that there is any social risk at all.

My daughter, Sarah, was born with ownership of her message in her DNA. I can't claim that she inherited from me. She will always take the diplomatic side if asked her opinion or if placed in a social spot requiring her to state an allegiance. Her opinions are retained until she feels the risk has been mitigated. She has done this since she could talk. It's amazing.

CHAPTER 69

"I" MESSAGES

Character may almost be called the most effective means of persuasion.

—Aristotle

When you have a reaction to something another person says or does, recognize that reaction and let the other person know how you are affected, using a phrase which describes and takes ownership of your feelings, such as:

> "I feel left out sometimes when we are in a group of people
>   and you seem to ignore me."
> "I feel that you have doubts about my judgment."

Be specific and clear about wants and needs.

When asking something from another person, use simple statements that take ownership of what you want or need, such as:

> "I want to …"
> "I don't want you to …"
> "Would you …?"

I statements are how you can frame your opinion in your language and create adhesion, not dissension.

CHAPTER 70

BE DIRECT

If you have it and you know you have it, then you have it. If you have it and don't know you have it, you don't have it. If you don't have it but you think you have it, then you have it.

—*Jackie Gleason*

While I do teach many courses and workshops under the title "assertiveness," I thought it much more valuable in a book format to write about being direct. Assertiveness tends to work best as a teachable concept in-person. There's more room for application and trial and error of understandings.

Being direct, asks you to know your intended message and to then be deliberate and thoughtful about delivering that message to the correct person - without implications and free of insinuating others. This means if you have a message for "X," deliver it directly - don't tell everyone except "X" and don't tell "X" while in a group. Your communication will be diluted and potentially (mis)interpreted by both "X" and everyone else. Why expose yourself to this vulnerability in your communication? Being direct limits the social risk of such exposure and of you being the one who is out of turn.

While I must admit I get it, there are those amongst us who erroneously believe that it is easier to tell a group of people, where "X" is a member, when you want to get your message across. Unfortunately, you miss the opportunity of at least maintaining if not gaining the respect that comes with being direct. Your message is at serious risk of being diluted along the way, and the worst part is that "X" may not even acknowledge that the message is actually intended for her/his benefit. Not to mention irritating the other members of the group who are at a minimum disinterested and at the other extreme annoyed.

CHAPTER 71

IGNORANCE VERSUS INNOCENCE

Opinion is the medium between knowledge and ignorance.

—Plato

Ignorance is the lack or absence of knowledge or understanding

Innocence is being uninformed or unaware.

There are differences between these two words that are worth your attention. Being ignorant is how we all are when we do not know something. It is, unfortunately, laden with social stigma that is usually negative.

Innocence is not an absence of information; instead it is the state of being unaware of there even being information to have. The positive social stigma associated with innocence has limited value at work, don't you agree?

With this clarification, ignorance can often take on a much more prestigious role on-the-job.

I challenge you to figure out if you are working from a place of ignorance or innocence. And I equally challenge you to seek out to understand those with whom you are interacting are ignorant or innocent. Make a definite determination and then choose your words and actions accordingly. Makes much more sense now doesn't it?

CHAPTER 72

DESIRABLE DIFFICULTIES VERSUS UNDESIRABLE DIFFICULTIES

When adversity strikes, that's when you have to be the most calm. Take a step back, stay strong, stay grounded and press on.

—*LL Cool J*

The problems you want or the problems you don't want. They are still problems, aren't they?

Sometimes we can all benefit from a bit of rock-hard perspective being thrown at us.

As I get older, I am surprised (occasionally underwhelmed) by the new tricks the human body offers its owners as the years pass. Stuff changes. New stuff is where there was nothing before. Some familiar stuff looks remarkably different. Don't even get me started on gravity.

I remember once when I had completed a 2-hour lunch n' learn session with a group at the Mississauga Campus of the University of Toronto. There is a particular seafood shop I only get to when I am working in the West end of the city, and the Mississauga campus puts it right on my route home. Perfect. Following one such lunch n' learn session, I drive over to make my purchases. Once done, I make my way to the parking lot to unload my bags into the back of my car when, from behind, I see a young male staff member struggling to collect and assemble the stray shopping carts strewn throughout the parking lot.

I battled putting my bags into my trunk (I tend to buy a lot at this seafood shop because I don't get there very often). I watched this fellow struggle with the carts, all the while hoping he would turn around and offer to either help me or, at least, take my cart from me so I wouldn't have to push it over to the drop-off shelter myself. I finished loading the bags, turned back and saw that same fellow continue to struggle now facing me so I could clearly see that he was working without the lower half of his left arm and with a few oddly shaped, fingers at the end of his right arm. I caught myself staring. He smiled. I smiled back. I pushed my cart over to match-up with the ones he had lined up. He thanked me and continued to do his job. I got in my car and thought about my ridiculous difficulties of loading bags with two fully functional arms and hands and felt very small indeed.

I love it when the universe kicks me hard in the temple like that. I have the difficulties I would greatly prefer. Perspective sometimes comes from without rather than from within.

That same day, I drove my car home, thinking about this lesson of perspective and it lead to even more thinking. Here I was dwelling on my overall healthy, intact aging body when others have many more serious bodily issues to live with and negotiate. I was worried about gravity? How vain I am. How simple and self-centred could I be? Relativity is underrated.

What a day.

Thank you Universe.

CONCLUSION

The true test of one's mettle is how many times you will try before you give up.

—Stephen Richards

Mettle. Not medal. Not metal. But, mettle. Look it up if this seems fantastical to you. Yes, it is not a misspelling. Mettle. What could that possibly mean? You've heard it, and I'll bet most likely assumed it was medal or metal. "She was worth her mettle." Although perhaps medal worthy or even made of metal, it's mettle.

Mettle is a reference to one's ability to cope well with difficulties or to face a demanding situation. How do you prevail? How do you move forward? It usually suggests more than survival. Mettle suggests a spirited and resilient way in which you choose to cope with difficulties or a particularly demanding scenario. It is how you represent yourself when pushed by circumstances that you may not have predicted but certainly did not welcome.

Why am I concluding with mettle? Excellent question. Here is the equally excellent answer. At this very moment, you have completed some (perhaps all) of this book. Congratulations. That means you have many new insights into how you can muster up your mettle, get your soft skills in order and be more.

I dare you.

Enjoy.

ABOUT THE AUTHOR

Diana Kawarsky, MA—Professional Overview

Diana is President of The Soft Skills Group Inc.(www.tssg.ca). She is a senior training & development professional offering 20 years of experience in delivery, design & consulting with Fortune 500 companies, Universities & Colleges in Canada, the USA, and Europe.

An energetic, results-oriented consultant, Diana takes great pride in influencing the human side of business. She has delivered training for banks, investment firms, law firms, and wealth management corporations. Diana has worked with organizations in many industries —including finance, telecommunications, health care, manufacturing, transportation, natural resources, not-for-profit and governments and crown corporations. Her experience has breadth from working with a variety of professionals from new hires to seasoned executives at the C-Suite level—totaling over 18,000 clients to date.

In addition to her corporate work, Diana teaches regularly at the Schulich Executive Education Centre (SEEC) of the York University where her feedback ranks her within the top 3% of all faculty. She also teaches frequently at the University of Toronto, the University of Ontario Institute of Technology, the University of Guelph, and McMaster University. Earlier in her career, Diana worked at a senior managerial level in corporate people management including training and development responsibilities.

She is intuitive with a passion for helping people and organizations perform. Diana completed formal studies at the University of Toronto, Simon Fraser University and Athabasca University, specializing in adult learning, human systems, organizational development and business management. She has both an undergraduate degree (BA) and a Master's Degree (MA). She has also earned the designation of Certified Coach Practitioner.

She is certified to use profiling tools such as the MBTI®, Emotional Intelligence Quotient (EQ-i), True Colors®, and Life Skills. She is an avid writer on business and career success-oriented topics, as well as a popular conference speaker.

Diana Kawarsky—Personal Overview

Outside of a dog, a book is a man's best friend. Inside of a dog it's too dark to read.

—Groucho Marx

I am a person who has not fit into any narrative neatly for very long in my life. Hegemonies have come and gone and yet I have managed to turn out all right—if I do say so myself—so far.

People often say I am well spoken, thoughtful and a captivating public speaker. I do try to live up to this feedback.

I earned my Master's Degree while building both my business and family. I have honed my people skills through both keen observation and application of best practices, an unexpected but welcomed by-product of a limited emotional repertoire as a youth and as an intentionally engaged adult.

I am a fantastic wife, an amazing mother, a well-respected and sought after professional, an OK friend, a mediocre in-law and a nuisance of a passenger (plane, train, boat, car—you name it).

I am also well spoken, and pretty comfortable with my personal levels of assertiveness. I can be an unexpectedly loud introvert.

Glad to meet you.

CPSIA information can be obtained
at www.ICGtesting.com
Printed in the USA
LVHW041924230719
625023LV00002B/281/P